the TRAP of SILENT DEPRESSION

MY UNTOLD STORY OF REJECTION, DEPRESSION, AND DELIVERANCE

GREAT CHURCH MINISTRIES

©2018 by Dan Walters

Published by Great Church Ministries ©2018
*The Trap of Silent Depression: My Untold Story of Rejection, Depression, and Deliverance /
Dan Walters*

ISBN: 978-1-947671-24-9

All scripture quotations are from the Holy Bible, New International Version (NIV) 1973, 1978, 1984 by International Bible Society

All rights reserved. No part of this publication may be reproduced, distributed, or transmitted in any form or by any means, including photocopying, recording, or other electronic or mechanical methods, without the prior written permission of the publisher, except in the case of brief quotations embodied in critical reviews and certain other noncommercial uses permitted by copyright law. For permission requests, write to the publisher at the address below:

Email: greatchurchministries@gmail.com
Phone: (513) 235-8833

Cover & Interior Design: D.E. West / ZAQ Designs - Dust Jacket Creative Services

Printed in the United States of America

GREAT CHURCH MINISTRIES

DEDICATION

This book is dedicated to my loving wife, Darlene, who has been my constant companion and faithful partner in ministry, who also suffered alongside me in silence yet stood by me in the darkest days of my depression with unconditional love. She provided me the daily inspiration to hold on until happier days arrived.

And to my three wonderful sons, Danny Scot, Darren Joel, and Devon Paul, who are witnesses to the miraculous healing power of Jesus in their father's life. And to my daughters-in-law, Jenny and Jody, whom I love dearly, and to my grandchildren, Makenzie Lea and Silas Daniel, who are the joy of my life and are all serving Jesus Christ their Savior today.

I also dedicate this book to the pastors and spouses and all who find themselves trapped in the dark pit of depression and despair and are suffering in silence–and to those who feel the pain of rejection and betrayal by their significant others as well as a poor self-image and inferiority. Perhaps you suffer from fear of failure and it seems that all hope is gone. *Look up–help is on the way!*

TABLE of CONTENTS

Dedication III
Introduction.. VII

1. The Call from Hell's Door 1
2. The Unseemly Rejection 7
3. The Inextinguishable Fire 13
4. Whoever Put the "Good" in "Goodbye"?................. 21
5. A Man Sent from Heaven–His Name Was Dave 25
6. Back Home and Waiting on God 33
7. God Stirs Our Nest Again 39
8. Pastor Crushed by Church Doors........................... 45
9. Satan Declares War.. 53
10. Be Careful About What You Ask For 63
11. The Merge, the Submerge, and the Emerge 75
12. Help Me, Lord–I'm Falling................................... 89
13. Carried Away in the Spirit 101

Conclusion... 107
Appendix.. 113
About the Author... 119

INTRODUCTION

Why, my soul, are you downcast?
Why so disturbed within me?
Put your hope in God, for I will yet praise him,
my Savior and my God
(Psalm 42:11)

I don't ever remember a time when I did not attend church regularly. I'm thankful for the Christian heritage passed down from Mom and Dad to me and my four brothers and two sisters.

My mother and father were hardworking parents, whose work included full time factory jobs along with a full-time side job raising a garden large enough to feed seven kids. I have memories as a child of Dad throwing me up onto the back of a mule that was hooked to a plow, and with that mule and plow he would till the ground and make furrows to plant seeds. Mom and Dad would can the garden vegetables each fall so that we would have good country eatin' during the winter and spring. Dad would always say during canning season, "We'll eat what we can, and what we can't eat we'll can."

In spite of the demands placed upon the parents of a large family, somehow we managed to attend church regularly three services per week plus Sunday School. I learned as a child that God was at the top of our priority list–He would be first at all times. I still have a picture of me when I was eight or nine years old wearing a cowboy hat and shirt with a Sunday School card sticking out of my shirt pocket. I can remember falling asleep during the long services and waking up to people singing and shouting and praying around the altar as the power of God would fall and meet people's needs. Those were the days!

It's no wonder I would develop a tender conscience toward God that would take me into my teen years when I met a beautiful young girl by the name of Darlene with curly auburn hair and hazel eyes who sang like an angel and loved the Lord with all her heart. I fell in love with her at first sight and soon through persistence won her love for me. I was fourteen and she was twelve, but God was joining together two loves that He would use for the next fifty-nine years for his glory in Kingdom-building through singing, teaching, and preaching.

We always loved God, and in time the years of childhood turned into adolescence and eventually into young adulthood and then marriage. It was about this time that I felt a burning desire to preach God's Word. I had a great pastor who could preach and dramatize a message or story and make it so real that you felt as if you were right there. I wanted to pass this convicting spirit on to others who did not know the gospel and saving power of Christ. It was at the end of my teen years, just recently married to my sweetheart, that God began dealing with my heart to answer His call to ministry, which would begin a long journey from the church family where my wife, Darlene, and I grew up, through a maze of misunderstandings and misinterpretations that would lead us into territory where battles between God and Satan are fought.

This is what this book is about. *The Trap of Silent Depression* is about the personal story of my call to ministry and the unexpected rejection by my significant others which had a devastating effect in my life. I would consequently fight the ongoing battle of low self-esteem, inferiority, and the fear of failing while seeking approval from my significant others. This would culminate in years of "silent depression" which could not be shared with anyone, and I would need a miracle to be rescued from the aloneness of the dark pit of mental and emotional anguish and suffering. Many pastors (and others) today are experiencing the same battles, and you have a story much like mine. May my story give you hope as you seek to escape your own trap of silent depression.

Numerous studies reveal that the demands placed on clergy put pastors at a far greater risk for depression than individuals in other occupations. Many pastors and wives feel unqualified to perform the pastor's role, and most of these experience ongoing conflict in their church. Couple this with the fact that pastors and wives feel as if they live in "glass houses" and are being judged by a higher moral standard than their members.

As if that were not enough, consider the stress placed upon the pastor as he or she must lead the church from a modern to a postmodern congregation, which in itself causes division and often loss of close friends. Fuller Institutes states that approximately 1,300 pastors leave the ministry every month and that only one out of ten will retire as pastors. I believe one reason for this is that underneath the stress and unrealistic demands of ministry, as some studies show, approximately thirty-five percent of all pastors are dealing with fear of inadequacy and depression, of which many suffer in silence–alone with no one to talk to about it.

I recall a pastor friend of mine standing on the front door steps of his church one day whistling away. I asked him, "Why are you whistling?" and with a look of pain on his face he replied, "To keep from crying." I did not offer any advice or solutions, because I too was trying to keep from crying.

However, today I can offer some great advice from experience–take heart and do not be discouraged! God knows who you are and where you live. He walks the dark hills and valleys, and He wants to deliver you from your trap of silent depression. He says in Isaiah 65:24, "Before they call I will answer; while they are still speaking I will hear." Lift up your head–help is on the way!

While depression is part of the human condition, the National Institute of Mental Health estimates that sixteen million Americans have experienced at least one serious episode, and the World Health Organization estimates that 350 million people worldwide suffer from depression. Depression is more than just feeling "down"–it can be caused by changes in brain chemistry. Research tells us that other factors contribute to the onset of depression, including genetics, changes in hormone levels, certain medical conditions, stress, grief, or other difficult life circumstances.

My story comes from the perspective of pastoring for thirty-nine years. I learned personally that pastors are not exempt from the dark valley of depression even though they rarely admit it, which only compounds the problem. Many sources today confirm that the rate of pastors dealing with depression is higher than that of the general population. Many reasons can account for this, one of which is low self-esteem. A person with low self-esteem feels unworthy, incapable, and incompetent. Pastors in general who have low self-esteem and a poor self-image will risk falling into the trap of comparing themselves with others, which causes an inability to be fair to themselves. There's also the lack of financial security or the ability to manage the personal day-to-day obligations, which creates anxiety and emotional turmoil.

Then there is the lack of necessary down time to balance church life with home life. If that's not enough, vacations for the pastor and his family are often low on the priority list due to lack of funds or time constraints. One of the major culprits causing depression among pastors is the unrealistic demands placed upon them, often coupled with unkind criticisms, which take a toll on their marriages and children. And the enemy of the Cross, Satan, is also the enemy of God's people and especially of those pastors who have been called to preach the truth of His Word. Pastors are a main target for Satan's schemes, and he works in any way he can—including depression—to discourage, defame, and defeat the man or woman of God.

Depression often manifests itself in feelings of severe despondency, dejection, and underlying anger. A pastor often deals with depression in silence for fear of appearing weak to his or her congregation, peers, and the upper leadership of his or her denominational organization. Fear of failure is one of the main culprits of depression, manifesting itself as an unhealthy driver for someone to succeed, which in turn leads the person more deeply into the dark valley of despondency. Prolonged depression becomes a vicious cycle of helplessness and hopelessness and loneliness, with no apparent end in sight. This is the trap of silent depression.

It is not my intent to cover the medical side of depression, such as a "chemical imbalance" in your brain, which is a common and serious medical illness that negatively affects how you feel, think, and act. The phrase "medical imbalance" has become a buzzword today to explain mental health problems, including social anxiety. I too have been diagnosed with this buzz word, and I have personally experienced many of the common symptoms of "chemical imbalance" such as irritability, agitation or restlessness, and the inability to focus or concentrate. I have struggled with insomnia, weight gain, a lack of energy, and unexplainable anger and crying spells. However, there are other deeper causes for depression that are more difficult to diagnose or explain and often result in feelings of severe despondency and dejection that can dramatically interfere with a person's life and the lives of those he or she loves.

The good news is that some studies show that between eighty and ninety percent of people treated for medical depression find some level of relief or coping capability. However, my intent is to give hope to those who are feeling alone and angry with their situation and difficult circumstances in life. To those who feel trapped in silence with no one to talk to who can understand and relate to their pain and anxiety, allow me to remind you that God never loses sight of you and gives you a promise in Deuteronomy 31:8–"The LORD himself goes before you and will be with you; he will never leave you nor forsake you. Do not be afraid; do not be discouraged." And 1 Peter 5:7 says to "Cast all your anxieties on him because he cares for you." Remember that you are not on your journey alone–the one whose eye is on the sparrow watches over you today.

A significant other is a person whose relationship with another person is important to his or her well-being. This could be a spouse, relative, friend, teacher, or pastor who is held in high esteem. Rejection by significant others often gives birth to an underlying depression, which manifests itself in low self-esteem and the fear of failure. It is this fear of failure that often gives birth to an unhealthy motivation to succeed. Rejection and fear of failure must be overcome for us to be freed from the trap of silent depression.

For me the battle was long and the fight was intense, but when it seemed there was no hope and the battle would be lost, then it happened–victory! When the doctors had done all they could do, the dark cloud rolled back–and there was God!

1

THE CALL FROM HELL'S DOOR
The Battle for my Soul

The Spirit of the Lord is on me,
because he has anointed me to preach good news to
the poor. He has sent me to proclaim freedom
for the prisoners and recovery of sight for the blind,
to set the oppressed free
(Luke 4:18)

In 1964 I was nineteen years of age when I had a "Saul on the Damascus Road" experience (see Acts 9). However, the big difference was that rather than being on the road to the city of Damascus, I lay prostrate at the gates of hell, a place of evil, suffering, and a perpetual fire where the wicked are punished forever, a place "where there will be weeping and gnashing of teeth" (Matthew 13:50). One truth I learned about hell is that it is a place of conscious torment after death.

The Bible actually gives very few particulars about hell. We do know from Matthew 25:41 that it was originally intended for demonic spiritual beings, not people. Mark 9:43 and 9:48 compare it to a place burning. And in Matthew 22:13 hell is compared to darkness and is associated with intense pain and horror. I can personally vouch for the truth of the Bible, which does make clear that hell is real, it is eternal separation from God, and it is to be avoided at all costs–see Matthew 5:29-30. You don't want to go there–there's no way out!

Even having been raised in a Christian home and church, as so often is the case with others, I had chosen the wrong crowd to follow, and out of curiosity and peer pressure I tasted some of the forbidden fruit of the world. And just as Jesus said in His Word, "No one can serve two masters" (Matthew 6:24) and please them both.

My sins would soon find me out, and the next thing I knew I was spiraling out of control spiritually and physically. The steps of sin led me downward to the very door of Satan's home, and there I lay at the gates of the abyss. I was carried away in the Spirit, and like Paul, who said in 2 Corinthians 12:2, "Whether it was in the body or out of the body I do not know–God knows," it was real enough for me, so real that I cried out for God's mercy to save me from the darkness of the bottomless pit of billowing smoke and flames of fire and the screams of the multitudes of eternally lost souls. I lay there helpless and speechless, unable to speak, as I heard the demonic voice of Satan calling me to come into the pit of demons with the fire and black smoke and horrifying screams: "Come–you belong to me." I lay there petrified and paralyzed, unable to move as my life passed like a panorama before me while above me I heard the voice of God, my Creator and Savior, responding to Satan, "You cannot have him–he is Mine."

Think of it: God and Satan were actually arguing over my soul. That same battle goes on as well for your soul today. I cried silently out to God in my spirit, begging Him to save me from the eternal pit of suffering. As I lay in the floor on my stomach and in my own vomit, I pledged Him my life, my hands, my feet, my mouth, my all, and then all at once I felt as if a barrel of scalding hot water was dumped onto the top of my head, flowing down my entire body and covering my feet. I likened it to the experience Isaiah had when he was being commissioned by God in Isaiah 6:5-8:

> "Woe to me!" I cried, "I am ruined! For I am a man of unclean lips.". . . Then one of the seraphs flew to me with a live coal in his hand, which he had taken with tongs from the altar. With it he touched my mouth and said, "See, this has

touched your lips; your guilt is taken away and your sin atoned for." Then I heard the voice of the LORD saying, "Whom shall I send? And who will go for us?" And I said, "Here am I. Send me!"

The argument between God and Satan for my soul was over, and God had the final say. The battle was won and Satan was defeated. My sins were forgiven, and the darkness became light. As light filled the room, I came to myself and sat up on the floor just like the man in Mark 5:15 who was possessed by the legions of demons, "sitting there, dressed and in his right mind." This was my call to follow God and to preach His Word. This was my call to be a mouthpiece for Him and to be a finger to point the lost to the way that leads home. Hell's door had become my "sacred spot" where I yielded control of my body and soul to will of God for my life.

From this point I would seek to find my way into the ministry to which God was calling me. It would not be easy–Satan would use every obstacle, friend and foe, to block the way. However, I had been to hell's door and back, and nothing could stop me now. The invitational song that I had heard since I was a young boy all of a sudden became a life-saving reality.

All to Jesus I surrender;
All to Him I freely give.

I will ever love and trust Him,
In His presence daily live.
All to Jesus I surrender;
Humbly at His feet I bow,
Worldly pleasures all forsaken.
Take me, Jesus, take me now.

All to Jesus I surrender;
Make me, Savior, wholly Thine;
Let me feel the Holy Spirit,
Truly know that Thou art mine.

I surrender all.
I surrender all.
All to Thee, my blessed Savior,
I surrender all.

– Judson W. Van DeVenter

2

THE UNSEEMLY REJECTION

He was despised and rejected by mankind, a man
of suffering, and familiar with pain
(Isaiah 53:3)

Rejection is defined as "the refusal to accept or receive" and "the spurning of a person's affections." Jesus received the ultimate rejection, and any pain we'll ever experience in this life would pale in comparison with the pain He suffered when He was betrayed by His own disciples. He was found guilty of love in the first degree just before He was mocked, beaten, stripped naked, and led through the streets of Jerusalem in shame carrying His own cross. He walked up a hill called Golgotha outside the city, where He would willingly be crucified for our sins. Some say He died from a broken heart!

Rejection is painful, and being made to look silly and incompetent is a frightening experience. Also, risking everything by putting yourself out there only to be spurned can be devastating. And so it was the case with me.

My call to ministry would eventually lead me from the only church that I knew. It was a non-denominational church in Cincinnati, Ohio, with loving people and a church where the Spirit of God would often manifest himself to the congregation. It was a singing church with a Bible-preaching pastor. This is the church where my mother carried me in her arms as a newborn baby. This is where I spent my childhood and teen years growing up with friends and family. This is the sacred place where I was first introduced to Jesus as Savior and went down into the water to be baptized in a nearby river. This is where we celebrated every Christmas and Easter. This is the place where heaven came down and we experienced the Shekinah glory of God in our midst. It was common to see convicted sinners fall on their faces and repent and the sick in body miraculously healed.

This is where I met my wife and sweetheart, Darlene, and we fell in love at twelve and fourteen years of age. This is where as young teens my wife and I would sing down the glory of God and witness untold numbers of people being saved around the altars and added to the kingdom of God.

This is the place where my sweetheart and I would become husband and wife, where our children would be born, and where we would become the leaders of youth ministries and all their activities. It was the place where we were faithful and dependable supporters of the church, its ministries, and its leaders. What a great privilege and heritage that had been entrusted to us by God!

When I think of the church, I think of a family. First there is God's big family (1 John 3:1-2). When people hear the gospel, confess their sins, and place their faith and trust in Jesus Christ, they are at that moment born into God's kingdom (family) as His children and become heirs with Him for eternity (Romans 8:14-17). Second, part of God's big family is the local church family (household of faith) made up of personal family members and friends who laugh and cry together, caring for each other's needs (Galatians 6:10). We are literally one local fellowship of loving family members. It's true–loving family members are usually very protective of each another. However, loving family members have problems too, and one of the problems within a close family is that "'close' can become 'closed'!" In other words, they know how to hurt each other, and there are no hurts that can match the pain of being hurt by those you hold in high esteem and look to for your own self-worth. This is why "church hurts" have caused so much damage and casualties along the way. Many Christians who once rose to call Christ blessed have become a statistic in the heap pile of the anger and bitterness of church hurts.

Often these church family hurts come from misunderstandings and misinterpretations and are bred by familiarity. Sometimes family members do not recognize the gifts potential in their brothers and sisters that complete strangers do. Then there are times when family members feel threatened by other family members for one reason or another, and so it was in the case of my call to ministry. After all, I was just a young married guy, still a teen, and much like Jesus of Nazareth in Mark 6:4, where He said, "A prophet is not without honor except in his own town, among his relatives and in his own home." Because of this truth Jesus could not do many miracles in His own hometown.

This was somewhat true for me. It is easy to see from a family standpoint that it would be difficult to encourage or even accept a loved family member to leave home (the church) especially when he or she is needed to carry on some very important chores at home (the ministries). Therefore, when I made the proclamation of my call to the leadership of the church family, it was met with an unseemly rejection and, yes, even ridicule, manifesting itself in much pain, confusion, and discouragement.

Being so young and inexperienced and totally unaware of how to proceed forward with my call to ministry, I found this deep rejection by my significant others driving me into a trap of silence, and it became the seed of a poor self-image and an underlying depression that would remain silent for the next several years. I still have the image of two of my significant others, whether intentionally or not, coming to my home one evening and ridiculing me and beating me down with condescending words that left me so devastated when they departed my home that I laid on my living room couch and wept bitterly until late that evening, vowing that I would never put myself out there again for that kind of belittling treatment and rejection. The trap for silent depression had been set!

For the next twelve years I was too fearful of more rejection to mention my call to anyone again, except once at age twenty-six to my wife, and even then it was in the form of a letter. Even though Satan tried to extinguish my fire, God always left a burning ember in my heart to remind me of the promise I had made to Him twelve years earlier at the doorway of hell. I would experience ongoing spells of suppressed depression and anger over my rejected call, However, my wife and I continued our regular schedule of ministry responsibilities at our home church. After all, it was the only church family we knew and dearly loved.

An anonymous author wrote, "It's often said, 'Follow your heart.' I did, and it got broken. However, every time I thought I was being rejected from something good, I was actually being re-directed to something better."

3

THE INEXTINGUISHABLE FIRE

If I say, "I will not mention him or speak anymore in his name," his word is in my heart like a fire, a fire shut up in my bones. I am weary of holding it in; indeed, I cannot
(Jeremiah 20:9)

God's gifts and his call are irrevocable
(Romans 11:29)

Though I had kept my rejected call silent for twelve years, by the time I was thirty-one years of age the fire of my call could no longer be contained. My wife and I were serving as youth directors in my home church, and we were having wonderful success in our monthly Friday night evangelistic gatherings. We would sing and pray around the altar and were growing in our relationships with God. Teens were inviting their friends to the Friday night service, and many were receiving Jesus as their Lord. We were experiencing a real moving of the Holy Spirit among the youth. These are some of my fondest memories yet today. Many of these young people grew up and dedicated their lives to the work of the Kingdom and continue to reproduce their lives in the lives of others today.

It was during this time that that the burning of my call began to rekindle once again. It was like a fire shut up in my bones, and if I didn't tell it I believe the rocks would have cried out! Therefore, I was compelled to express to the pastor once again that God was calling me to preach His Word. I had been employed by the Ford Motor Company for many years by this point, and I was totally satisfied with my occupation; my only intention was perhaps to hold youth revivals and evangelize the young in a greater way than before. However, for whatever reason, as before, twelve years earlier, that painful word *rejection* raised its ugly head again. Sometimes our enemy uses the people we love the most who are unaware that they are roadblocks and obstacles to a greater cause that God is calling us to.

This time there was no outright rejection of my call, but the earlier "direct rejection" of twelve years earlier was replaced by another form of rejection known as pacification and appeasement. Intentionally or not, the quelling of my call was put into action. My pastor drove me to a Christian Bible college in Ohio, and I was under the impression I was going to be enrolled in a course of study that would begin to prepare me for my call to ministry. I remember how thrilled I was as we drove toward the college—at last I was getting on tract to answering my call from God. I thanked God in my spirit over and over again as we headed up the interstate and drew nearer to our college destination.

Once we arrived, we toured the campus and met the dean of the college. I was as excited as a kid at Christmas, in awe as I was introduced to some of the college staff and learned all about their history. I realized that since I had a full-time occupation, with a wife with three young children, I would not be privileged to be an on-campus resident. But just to think that I would be able to study home courses from a Christian college and prepare myself to do what God was calling me to do was totally enough to satisfy the longing in my heart and the hunger in my soul to learn and prepare.

After the campus tour, with my heart still beating out of my chest, my pastor drove me to a Christian bookstore nearby that he wanted to visit, just down the road from the college. Once we arrived and just before we exited the car, he turned to me and said, "Now, Dan, I've been talking to my son, and we've been thinking that what you really need is to take a Christian worker's course to learn more how to a witness and give Bible studies and such, and you really don't need to get involved in anything else."

What? I didn't even see it coming. I felt as if I had been sucker punched! This was a crushing blow to my spirit, and I felt myself go silent with unbelief and dismay, and the same rejection that I experienced twelve years earlier was fresh and alive again.

A happy heart makes the face cheerful, but heartache crushes the spirit (Proverbs 15:13).

By the time we entered the door, my countenance was all the way to the bottom. I had received the ultimate blow, and my self-esteem was at its lowest point ever. I felt betrayed, belittled, and spurned. In today's terminology as found in the Urban Dictionary, I felt "punched," a modern-day word for *tricked.* I remember my pastor telling the store clerk, "Let him have anything he wants, and put it on my bill." The clerk asked me what I wanted, and totally dejected, I replied, "Just anything you feel will help me to be a better witness for Christ," and I returned home that day with a bag full of Christian worker's materials that had very little meaning to me in regard to God's call on my life.

My dreams were shattered that day, and I believe "rejection"–the spurning of a person's affections–is one of the early seeds that produces silent depression in so many pastors and people today. I was learning an important lesson through the rejection by my significant others, and that is that sometimes God has to hurt us in order to help us!

How else could I ever have been able to follow His plan for my life, which included leaving the only church family I had ever known? If had not been broken enough to turn to Him who had been preparing the way forward all along, the outcome could have been tragically different today.

The Bible says in Proverbs 20:24, "A person's steps are directed by the LORD."

My trip to the Christian Bible college that ended in rejection in the form of pacification, appeasement, and a broken heart was not in vain. After all, now I knew where I could go for help and guidance, and someone there could direct me in the path forward to answer God's calling on my life. I made a trip to the Bible college on my own, and there I met one of the staff members in the admissions office, who enrolled me in a ministerial home-study course with the college. The Lord had directed my steps, and I was ecstatic with overwhelming emotions of joy and happiness. I was on my way to somewhere, and God was leading me. It was an exciting day!

Now it was time to prepare, and my first home study course was on homiletics–the art of preparing and preaching sermons, by Whitehall. I was so unlearned and had never before even heard the word *homiletics* and did not have a clue as to what it even meant. I often joked that I thought homiletics was a vegetable. Sure, I would have much rather taken a beginner's course in the studies of the Old and New Testaments; however, if they wanted me to study homiletics, so be it. I proudly carried my textbook every day with me to the Ford Motor Company, where I worked as an assembler. And not having a mentor or professor to teach me, I prepared myself for the test in the only way that I could—by memorizing the definition of every word in the index. Yes, you heard me right! It took me six long months of utilizing every break on the assembly line, every lunch hour, and every spare moment at home, where my wife would take care of our three children and give me study blocks of quiet time for study. Finally, after six months of memorizing the index definitions, I was ready to take the test. It had been so long since the college had heard from me that I'm sure they must have wondered if I had given up the whole idea of my calling. However, I would make my way back to the Bible college, and as I sat there in the dean's office, he administered to me the test on homiletics. Thankfully, there were enough test questions asked from the words listed in the index of the textbook that I pulled a B+ on the exam. I was so proud of my accomplishment and I could not wait to get back home and tell my wife. However, it dawned on me that at this pace I would be an old man before I graduated from the pastor's course of study. This was a beginning, though, and unknowingly to me, God was preparing my next step for the future—and it was coming soon.

During this time the situation began heating up at my home independent church. Whispers that I was enrolled in the course of ministerial studies were spreading throughout the congregation. I felt as if I were a secret agent for the Lord. While this was becoming big news, it also was becoming a point of contention. Unknowing to me, some of the church members were wondering if I would eventually become my pastor's assistant or even the next pastor, which was never my plan nor had it ever even entered my mind. The pastor had two sons who would logically be in line to be successors to their father's work and ministry.

Some of the church members began asking me about my call and my course of ministerial studies. Therefore, to quell the whisperings, one Sunday I announced to the congregation that God was calling me to ministry and that I had begun the course of study and did not know specifically what He was calling me to do or where, asking them to pray for me. There–I had said it!

At this point, due to misunderstandings, conflict begin to grow with the leadership of the church, and relationships were severely strained. I was given mixed signals between encouragement and discouragement regarding my call, and after approximately a year and a half of very intense and strained relationships, God spoke to my wife and me and said, "Enough! It's time!" After spending our childhood, our teen years, and our young adult years with the only pastor and congregation we had ever known, we made the prayerful and sure decision to say goodbye to all we had ever known and loved. And like Abraham, we did not have any idea where we were going–but God knew, and He would soon reveal it to everyone.

4

WHOEVER PUT THE "GOOD" IN "GOODBYE"?

"They all wept as they embraced him
and kissed him. What grieved them most was his
statement that they would never see him again.
Then they accompanied him to the ship"
(Acts 20: 37-38)

Even if you know what's coming, you're never prepared for how it feels.

The handwriting was on the wall. The time had come for my family and me to step out by faith from the familiarity and security of home and trust God to lead us in His pre-ordained plan for our future. My wife and I had been earnestly seeking God's leading in our lives for some time, and on Saturday, April 22, 1978, God spoke to both of us in prayer that it was time to move out and move on. As the writer of Hebrews 11:8 said about Abraham, he "obeyed and went, even though he did not know where he was going."

On Sunday morning, April 23, 1978, my wife and I got up early and agreed, after praying the evening before and sleeping on the word that God had given us, that it was time to leave our church of childhood and young adult years. Our family got dressed, and we arrived at the church as usual, following our regular format of Sunday School, worship, special singing, and preaching. It started as a stressful morning for me personally, because I was the teacher of the teen class, and I knew that this would be the last time I would be teaching them—and due to the circumstances I would not have the privilege to say an appropriate farewell.

Ecclesiastes 3:1, 4-5 says, "There is a time for everything . . . a time to weep and a time to laugh, a time to mourn and a time to dance . . . a time to embrace and a time to refrain from embracing." This was definitely a time to weep and mourn and a time to embrace. Therefore, at the close of the class and unable to say a formal farewell, I stood at the classroom door, and as the students departed the room, I hugged each one and told him or her, "I love you." They sensed that something was out of the ordinary, but no questions were asked. Unfortunately, that would be the last time I would stand before the wonderful group of teens that God had privileged me and my wife to love and serve.

The worship service started and as usual. My wife and I sang a special song before the pastor's message, as we had done since we were teenagers. We knew that God was leading us out and that this would be the last song we would ever sing to the church family whom we had loved all our lives. The song we sang was "I'll See You in the Rapture," which refers to the coming of the Lord as described in 1 Thessalonians 4:13-18. It was our way of saying to our church family that if we never meet again down here, there's another meeting place in the air when Jesus calls for His bride to rise, and we "will be caught up together with them in the clouds to meet the Lord in the air" (verse 17).

Even if you know what's coming, you're never quite prepared for how it feels. The congregation sensed something wasn't just right, but there would be no opportunities for questions. Following the morning sermon we waited for the pastor to finish his conversations with other parishioners until at last only he and we were left standing face to face. I said to him, "Pastor, God has been talking to Darlene and me about our future, and he has confirmed to us in prayer that it is time for us to move on from our home church and follow His will regarding my call to ministry."

Without hesitation, yet with a familiar strain, he replied, "You have to do what you have to do." He asked me where I thought I would go. My reply was that I did not know but that I believed that the God who had called me would also lead me forward. I believe we both welcomed the relief from a long-strained relationship. This was more affirmation that God was indeed calling us to another work for His kingdom, and it felt so right. We left that Sunday morning, and while walking to our car we experienced an inward witness that God would not allow us to return to this place again. We felt a mixture of sadness, relief, and excitement that at last we knew we were following the will of God for our future–but where?

I would soon learn that the teen class I had taught for several years had prepared a surprise appreciation party for me and my wife that evening at church, but we would not be there to receive their efforts of love–we were gone. I wonder whoever put the "good" in "goodbye"– I cried!

A farewell is necessary before you can meet again. And meeting again is certain for those who are part of God's family. Our hearts were meant for fellowship, love, and relationship. How blessed I was to have something that made saying goodbye so hard!

5

A MAN SENT FROM HEAVEN – HIS NAME WAS DAVE

There was a man sent from God whose name was John (John 1:6)

Relieved from the ongoing strained relationships yet reeling from the recent rejection by my significant others, I soon found that it didn't take long for the enemy, Satan, to begin his dirty work by causing confusion and doubt to come into my mind. I began to question, "How could this be God when it hurts so bad?" The seeds of silent depression planted years earlier by rejection had already taken root, and now the latest incident of rejection simply added pain upon pain.

My wife and I sat in our home on a Sunday afternoon without a church, without a church family, and without friends with whom to share our feelings. There was no going-away party, no hugs, no well wishes, no prayers, no thank-you cards, no we'll-miss-you tears, no support. It was as though we had simply been "cut off" with no identity and no direction. Satan swept over me with a spirit of coldness and fear, challenging my faith with "what if" questions. What if God doesn't reveal our next step? What if this and what if that? This would be the first Sunday night service, other than on rare occasions, that we would be absent. They will know something drastic is wrong. What if they don't understand? What if they feel hurt and betrayed–as I did? The pity party was on big time, and my frame of mind was ideal for Satan to move in as he does when we are at our most vulnerable. I felt trapped in my despondency and dejection. Had I done the right thing? *Where are You, God? Help me, please!* I was so sure this morning–but now I don't know. *Help me, God–please!*

My wife broke into the conversation I was having with myself and asked "Where are we going to church this evening?" "What?" I replied. Since we were used to attending church twice on Sunday, this was her main concern. However, I was being tempted by Satan to take a few months away from it all and try to figure out what had just happened. After all, Satan reminded me, this was not the way it should have been. Sometimes Satan appears to make sense of things, and he just about had me convinced when the phone rang. It was a call from God—well, actually it was from a young man named Dave. "There was a man sent from God whose name was Dave." He was one of my teen converts from several years earlier and was on fire for God. He had moved from the Cincinnati area to northern Kentucky, on the southern side of the Ohio River, and we hadn't talked to each other in a long time. He started: "Hey, Dan—I was just thinking of you and Darlene. How are you doing these days?"

I replied "Not so good today, Dave. We just left our church this morning after thirty-three years."

Dave knew this was extreme and said, "What? No way!" After filling him in on a few details that led up to our leaving, he graciously invited me and my wife to his home church in Covington Kentucky, the First Church of the Nazarene. "Hey, Dan—come. We have a special singing group here tonight, The Mowry Family. It will be good for you."

"I'm sorry, Dave," I replied. "I just want to take some time off and clear my head, but thanks anyway for the invitation, and thanks for calling and keeping in touch." We ended our conversation, and I went back to my pity party.

While I was busy focusing on *me* enumerating the many injustices I felt I didn't deserve, my wife had only one thought rolling around in her head, and that was where she would be going to church tonight. She blurted out, "Honey, if you're not going to church tonight, then I'm going to meet Dave in Covington and go to church with him."

That drove me temporarily insane, and I said, "No, you're not going to meet Dave in Covington and go to church with him. It would not look good for you to be riding around with another man in Covington, much less showing up at a church service with him. You're still my wife, so I'll just go with you!" I picked up the phone and called Dave back and said, "Dave, we've had a change of heart–Darlene and I will be visiting your church this evening."

Dave began praising the Lord, saying, "Dan, I've been on my knees praying that you would change your mind. The service begins at six–I'll see you there." God sent a man from heaven–his name was Dave–and my pity party was over. God was leading once again.

We arrived at the church in Covington a few minutes before 6 PM to be greeted at the door by a man named Hubert. I'll never forget his genuine smile and welcoming spirit–it was indeed impressive and just what I needed for that moment. Every church ought to have a greeter like Hubert. We entered the beautiful brick building foyer and made our way into the sanctuary with stained-glass windows, padded pews, high wood ceilings, and carpeted floors. It was a new and strange experience for my wife and me.

The home church we had just left had been a converted storefront that had served previously as a town bar. The sanctuary seats were three hundred-plus individual wood theater seats, the ceiling was of acoustic square blocks, and the floor consisted of one-square-foot linoleum tiles. The back wall of the platform had a painted life-size picture from John 4–the woman at the well–and reminded everyone that if we would drink from the water that Jesus gives, we would never thirst again. From the time I was a child I had loved that picture. There was room for a piano on the left side of the stage and a small organ on the right side, with three choir pews to the right of the organ. In the center of the stage there was room enough for acoustic, electric, and steel guitars, along with a base fiddle to complete the church band. Wow! Did they ever have some great music! The pulpit had a sign across the front that read "Jesus Saves." These were memories of the only church I ever knew and loved, and they were flooding my mind. Now I was sitting in this big elaborate temple as a coldness swept over me and I began questioning once again, "What have I done?"

The service started, and the Mowry Family began singing their first song when the heavens opened and God poured out His blessings and peace upon me and my wife. The coldness, the confusion, and the fear were all dispelled in the presence and grace of God and replaced with tears of joy and assurance for our future.

Peace, peace! wonderful peace,
Coming down from the Father above!
Sweep over my spirit forever, I pray,
In fathomless billows of love.

–W. D. Cornell

My wife and I sat and cried throughout the whole service, and at the close we shook hands with a young couple sitting in the pew behind us who had been shedding tears all evening as well. I asked if they attended church there regularly, and they said they were first-time visitors, too, who had just left their church with a broken heart that morning after thirty-two years and were looking for place to attend. When God gives assurance of His will, he does it in a way to leave no questions. He was bringing broken hearts together that day, and we would soon see that He would intertwine our futures together so that His plan for us would soon be realized. We left First Church that evening with a much-needed outpouring from heaven, and Hubert, the greeter who had welcomed us at the door, invited us to come back again. However, in my mind I had no intention to return to this beautiful edifice.

The following morning my wife and I headed south to Florida to fulfill a previous revival and singing commitment for a Nazarene church there. Here we were living in Cincinnati with no church to attend, heading down south to participate in evangelistic services in another Nazarene congregation. It was in this revival that our singing about Jesus to others actually became a revival for us. God moved in and spoke clearly to us that He was in charge and that the next step in His plan for us would soon be made known. It was time to close the book on our previous home church and all that was behind us and begin a new chapter in our lives. Although we did not know what God would do next for us, He assured us that He would lead the way if we would just follow. And follow we did.

6

BACK HOME AND WAITING ON GOD

The revelation [vision] awaits an appointed time; it speaks of the end and will not prove false. Though it linger, wait for it; it will certainly come and will not delay.
(Habakkuk 2:3)

It seems that the more we want something the harder it is to wait—and we even get impatient with God. However, waiting on Him involves so much more than just waiting. It transforms our character, creates anticipation, and builds dependency upon God.

It would be two weeks before we would return home from our Florida revival, and I would return to work at the

Ford Motor Company where I had been employed for the past fourteen years. I was working the midnight shift one night, often referred to as the graveyard shift, when the machines in my department malfunctioned, resulting in my being sent home early after midnight. At approximately 1:30 I crawled into bed with my wife and immediately went to sleep, since this was an unusual and welcome treat for me. Sometime after 2:30 in the morning I was awakened by a storm with flashes of lightning and cracks of thunder, and my heart seemed to be beating out of my chest. I felt that God was speaking to me through the storm, so I got out of bed and hurried to an adjoining homemade reading and prayer room, where I began listening to God's voice speaking to my spirit.

The words He spoke to me would be life-changing and would head us on a path that He had already ordained for us to walk–they still burn in my memory as if it were only yesterday: "I want you to take your wife and children and return to Covington, Kentucky, First Church of the Nazarene. I am going to bless you there." I was in awe, almost too shocked to move. I was in the presence of God. He was talking to me and showing me where to put my foot down next. I could hardly breathe, and in the excitement I awakened my wife out of a deep sleep and told her what God had spoken and directed me to do. She sat up in the bed and asked, "Are you sure?"

I replied, "I'm sure." It was hard for us to grasp what God was doing, but we were willing to follow His directions.

The next Sunday, just as God had ordered, we pulled into the parking lot of First Church, walked up to the front doors, and there again stood Hubert the greeter with his "I'm so glad to see you" smile and said, "Welcome back, Dan and Darlene." I couldn't believe he remembered our names. It was a great Sunday service. We enjoyed the choir, the worship service, and the message by the pastor. Our children–Danny Scot, 8, and Darren Joel, 2 (a third son, Devon Paul, would be born one year later)–loved their new classes and friends, and we, who had been wandering around in the wilderness waiting on God's guidance, all at once knew we were at our new home, with our new church family and in the center of God's will!

Before leaving First Church that Sunday, I requested a meeting with the pastor to be set up. We met at the church on Monday morning, and I was hoping he could give me further guidance in continuing my education and my call to preach. It turned out that he and the congregation at First Church had been praying for God to send a younger couple to help draw other young couples to the church. He himself had asked God when he saw us come in on Sunday morning, "God, is this the couple we've been praying for?" He shared with me the many needs the church had for an assistant pastor and showed me a church bus with only seven thousand miles but no driver to pick up inner-city children on Sundays. We talked about the possibilities of outreach and various in-house children, youth, and adult ministries, and walked through the facilities weeping and praising God for the opportunities to accomplish the Great Commission of Matthew 28. God was moving, He was doing a new thing–and it was time to move with Him!

The pastor helped me get enrolled in the pastoral track at Mount Vernon Nazarene College in Mount Vernon, Ohio, presented me with a local preacher's license, and recommended to the church board that I become his assistant pastor. Two weeks later I officially became the assistant pastor of Covington First Church of the Nazarene. Pastors who know how the Nazarene *Manual* works also know that this in itself was a miracle! When God is ready to move, He often gets it done overnight!

My wife and I spent our next three years working at First Church in ministry, and the congregation grew from less than a hundred to several hundred in a short span of time. Remember the young couple I spoke of earlier who had left their church after thirty-two years? Well, we worked side by side and hand in hand for Christ until the wife passed away from melanoma cancer. She is now in heaven cheering for us while her husband continues serving the Lord at the same church today.

I could have spent many more happy years at First Church, and I'll always cherish the special relationships we developed there, but God had other ideas, and another farewell was in the making. However, this time the bitterness of leaving would be tempered with sweetness and tears of love.

AUGUST 1978 - THE WALTERS FAMILY STANDING AT THE ENTRANCE DOORWAY OF COVINGTON FIRST CHURCH OF THE NAZARENE

JULY 1979 - DAN WALTERS HOLDING HIS NEWBORN SON, DEVON PAUL AND HIS LOCAL PREACHER'S LICENSE.

7

GOD STIRS OUR NEST AGAIN

*Every new beginning comes from some
other beginning's end. Like an eagle that stirs up
its nest and hovers over its young, that spreads its
wings to catch them and carries them aloft
(Deuteronomy 32:11)*

God, like the eagle, stirs our nest. Yesterday it was the place He wanted us to be–but today there is a new plan. He breaks up the nest, even though He knows it is dear to us, or perhaps *because* it is dear to us. Why? That He may get us onto His wings and lead us to a higher purpose for His glory.

Things were moving along at First Church just fine, and I was happy with my position as assistant pastor. I was enjoying the time and direction I had been given for the study toward my ministry education, and I was very content. My family was happy with their new church family, and we were very comfortable in our nest. Therefore, in the late winter of 1980 I was surprised to receive a call from the superintendent of the Southwestern Ohio District of the Church of the Nazarene asking if I would interview at a little church in Hamilton, Ohio. My immediate response was no. After all, I was satisfied to be where I was in my ministry nest. End of conservation, I thought.

However, one month later he called me again, saying God had definitely spoken to him in prayer directing him to ask me again to at least consider interviewing with this small church board in Hamilton before giving a definite no. I felt compelled to honor his sincere request and to test the waters to see if God was actually speaking. So I agreed, along with my wife, to meet for an interview with the church board—and that meeting would be another life-changing event.

It was a small church of approximately forty-five people located on the west side of Hamilton, near Cincinnati. My parents had visited family friends in that area when I was just a child, and for some reason that I cannot explain, I had a dislike for the Hamilton area. The interview took place in early January of 1981. It was a cold night, the ground was covered with snow, and in the darkness everything in the neighborhood including the church building itself appeared to be uninviting. However, we met with a small delegation from the church, who also happened to be the church board. We greeted each, and they shared their sincere need for a pastor-leader. They were kind and gracious and yet very discouraged. I saw them as lost sheep wandering around in the wilderness without a shepherd. These people had experienced the loss of four pastors in the past five years, who had all left them for one reason or another, and now they were extending a call for me to become their pastor.

Our hearts were touched, and when we left the interview that evening my wife and I could not speak about what we saw and felt but agreed to pray and fast for one week before discussing the issue again. Surely God would not call us to such a dysfunctional situation. We were so happy at First Church. We had been there only three years, and our children had adjusted well and made new friends. My wife and I had settled into our meager salary package, and we still lived in our little home on the west side of Cincinnati, just twelve miles across the Ohio River from First Church. I was also working on my fourth year of ministerial studies, and another move could not come at a worse time.

However, one week came and passed since the interview, and now it was time for my wife and me to come face to face to discuss whether or not God was calling us to the little church in Hamilton. We sat down at the dining room table in our little home, and I opened the conversation by asking my wife, "Well, what is God telling you?" We sat silently and just stared at each other until tears filled our eyes. I said to her, "I believe God is telling us that we have to go," and she nodded. With no need for further discussion, the decision was made at the end of our week of prayer and fasting. God had spoken, and there was nothing else to discuss. So like an eagle that stirs up its nest, Jesus was stirring our nest and calling upon us to follow Him once again.

I phoned the Southwestern Ohio district superintendent and informed him that I would accept the call to become the pastor to the little congregation in Hamilton, a city I had vowed never to live in. God does have a sense of humor, doesn't he? The next morning I informed my pastor at First Church that I had accepted a call from the Hamilton church, to which he replied, "Dan, you'll be moving down instead of up—please let me help you. I have contacts." He was genuinely concerned and well-meaning.

However, my reply to him was "I have a contact also, and He's already spoken to me—I have to go." I turned in my resignation to First Church, and on a Sunday morning thirty days later, my wife and I stood at the back sanctuary door. As the members of the congregation exited, we wept on each other's shoulders and bid our farewells until another day.

Someone once said, "Remember me and smile, for it's better to forget than to remember me and cry."

8

PASTOR CRUSHED BY CHURCH DOORS

We are hard pressed on every side, but not crushed
(2 Corinthians 4:8)

My wife and I were looking forward to our next assignment at the small Nazarene church in Hamilton, Ohio. It would be the first church where I would be the senior pastor, in this case the only pastor. On February 8, 1981, we arrived at the church with keys in hand to the front double doors. I felt a great measure of pride mixed with a great measure of apprehension. A combination of emotions and anxieties swirled around in my head. The "what if'" questions began consuming my thoughts. What if I don't succeed as a pastor? What if the people don't like us? What if we can't raise enough finances to pay the bills and my salary? What if the church can't afford medical insurance? I have three children, and I'm a diabetic. After all, the little church was taking in only about two hundred fifty dollars per week, and I had taken a fifty-percent decrease in salary from my previous position at First Church to come as their pastor–but still it would be a stretch for them.

And what if our children didn't like their new school? They had been attending a small community school in a safe environment where they walked to school and back home every day with friends. Now they would be standing at a dangerous intersection waiting for a school bus to transport them to their new elementary school set right in the middle of a steel factory town with a much less safe environment and culture. Adjusting to new teachers and making new friends and missing the old ones–what if?

Now everyone would be watching, and for the first time it became frighteningly obvious to me that I had to succeed, I had to make it all work, I could not fail, I was on my own, and the whole weight was on my shoulders. This dependency on myself created an unhealthy need to succeed and a real fear of failing, and the painful rejections of the past became so magnified in my mind that fear of failing would be the driving force that would soon lead me into a deep silent trap of depression. More on that later.

I took the keys with a feeling of achievement and unlocked the front double wood doors of the church. I pulled the handle to open the doors, and to my surprise both of them and the attached casings fell out into my arms. I struggled to hold up the heavy weight, and all I could imagine was the evening news headlines: "Nazarene pastor crushed to death by church doors." I claimed the promise in 2 Corinthians 4:8–"Hard pressed on every side, yet not crushed." Thankfully I survived, and my first building project was to secure the door casings with a hammer and nails. Many building projects would soon follow.

If that weren't enough, one board member phoned me to say that there were no longer forty-five people who would be attending the church. One week before we arrived approximately half of the people decided that they no longer wanted to be Nazarenes and left to start their own independent church. I felt like saying, "Well, bless God–tell me more!" And tell me more they did. When we pulled our U-Haul into the driveway of the parsonage, a man came running from across the church yard shouting, "Are you our new pastor?" I was hesitant to say yes, but I did. Without even introducing himself he blurted out, "We have a problem–our septic tank is overflowing and is piling up at the back exit door of the church!" I assured him that we also had another problem: I did not do septic tanks. I instructed him to call a septic tank company and have them take care of it. This was my first order of leadership and delegation skills.

We unloaded our U-Haul's first load into the parsonage and returned to Cincinnati to retrieve another load. By the time we had arrived back at the parsonage, someone had already come into the parsonage and rummaged through our personal items. The word eventually got back to us that we did not live any better than the other church people. In other words, "They're one of us." That was a big relief.

I was also informed that the church remained cold most of the winter months since the steam water pipes that heated the sanctuary had leaks in them and that the only way to bring up the heat was to bleed several water line valves before each service. My leadership skills kicked in again, and two hours before each service either I or a dear lay friend would climb into the attic of the church with a flashlight and a screw driver and crawl from one end to the other relieving trapped air from bleeder valves until the heat would rise enough for us to have a comfortable sanctuary. A comfortable sanctuary would be anything that reached fifty degrees and above.

The church windows were extremely drafty, enough so that one day I saw a bird squeeze into the sanctuary through a gap in one of them. Once again my building skills kicked in, and I delegated a group of men and women to foam up all the gaps in the window frames and replace all the cracked window putty. At last we would have a comfortable sanctuary warm and bird-free. If only we could replace the rubber matting on the floor with new carpeting, the ladies would be able to kneel and pray without tearing their hose or skinning their knees. However, that would have to wait for a while.

We were getting wins under our belt and beginning to believe in ourselves. The Spirit of God fell upon our services—souls were being saved and lives were being transformed. People began hearing about the moving of God upon our church and came to see what it was all about. After all, where there's smoke there's fire. We knocked on hundreds of neighborhood doors to invite families to our little family church. The church began to grow numerically, and finances followed people in. Our attendance grew from a handful of people to surpassing the 100 weekly average mark, and from there we never looked back. Many upgrades and remodeling projects followed—a roof replacement, an expanded sanctuary, new parking lots, and oh, yes—a new septic system.

Some of the greatest joys of my ministry and some of the greatest saints of God were at this little Nazarene church in Hamilton. Now our facilities were maxed out, and we needed more room for more people. These were exciting days for our ministry—and Satan didn't like it!

THE SMALL NAZARENE CHURCH IN HAMILTON, OHIO

1985 – THE SMALL NAZARENE CHURCH AFTER UGRADES

THE TRAP OF SILENT DEPRESSION

FAMILY PICTURE

9

SATAN DECLARES WAR

Put on the full armor of God, so that you can take your stand against the devil's schemes. For our struggle is not against flesh and blood, but against the rulers, against the authorities, against the powers of this dark world and against the spiritual forces of evil in the heavenly realms
(Ephesians 6:11-12)

While raising three boys, my wife and I were working as a team six days and six nights a week giving all our talents and energy to the ministries of the church, and Satan, our enemy, didn't like what he saw. Therefore, he strategized and schemed, sending his attack-ers to stop us. He often uses dark forces of evil to fight for him, and they often look simply like normal people.

Word came to us that a man and wife who were practicing the witchcraft of black magic were making Voodoo dolls in the likeness of me and my wife. Now, we're not talking Ken and Barbie here. Voodoo is witchcraft and the practice of magic, especially black magic—it is the use of spells and the invocation of evil spirits. It was revealed that they were sticking pins in the voodoo dolls in hopes that it would cause us pain and even putting them in a freezer in hopes that we would freeze to death. That may account for the extra cold winter that year—tongue in cheek.

The weapons we fight with are not the weapons of the world. On the contrary, they have divine power to demolish strongholds (2 Corinthians 10:4). Satan's attack by Voodoo didn't have a chance. He was defeated before he started. However, he never tires of trying!

The enemy put into action another strategy. I arrived one morning at my office at the church, next door to the parsonage, to find dozens of pornographic photographs scattered all over the church lawn and at my office door. How humiliating! Also, next to the highway approximately fifty feet from the office door, for all the drivers and passengers to see and read as they rode by, was a large white poster leaning up against the mailbox with large black letters reading, "Pastor Walters, take your ugly wife and stupid children and go back to Cincinnati where you came from. No one loves you around here." Not exactly words of encouragement, but it was obvious to me this was just another silly attack of the devil's minions.

A few weeks later a dear woman came to me and asked if she could compare the writing on the poster with the writing on a birthday card her ex-husband recently sent to her daughter. Bingo–it was a match! I took the poster and filed it with the Hamilton Police Department and advised them that if I turned up missing–here's the name of the man you want to question. Obviously he didn't kill me–I'm still here.

Satan's next plot would be an intimidation attack upon me and my family. On a Thursday night my wife and kids had just returned home when a trio of men came rushing in unannounced through our parsonage's front door. I guess you could call it a Satanic home invasion. They were filled with an evil spirit and threatening my life with physical harm. The spokesman for the three men stood nose to nose with me in the dining room of our home as evil, demonic words proceeded from his mouth–"The spirit of the Lord has sent me here." My wife and three children crouched underneath the kitchen table for protection, and one of our kids cried out in fear: "Mommy, are they going to kill us?" Meanwhile, in the adjoining dining room the three men summoned me to come outside so they could do their demonic business. The situation was grave, and the only thing I could think of was to rebuke the demonic spirits in the three men as Jesus did the demon-possessed man of the Gerasenes (see Luke 8).

I don't know whether or not you believe Christians are provided the authority to rebuke the devil as Jesus did, but when you come face to face with a demonic spirit and your family's lives depend on it, you'll try anything. So I did! I began crying out with a loud voice three times in the midst of his evil guttural chanting, "The spirit of God has sent me here." Each time I would returned with a more powerful chant–"I rebuke you in the powerful name of Jesus," and after the third time the man that I was face to face with stopped his evil chanting, stepped backward, dropped his limp arms to his side, his face turned to an ash white, and he asked, "What did you say?"

I repeated once again, "I rebuke you in the powerful name of Jesus for coming into the house of His servant and threatening his life. In Jesus' name I command you to leave this home now." Without a word the three men turned slowly and walked out the same door they had just invaded, and I was so emboldened with the mighty power of the Holy Ghost that I followed them out to their car and said to them, "If you men ever want to know Jesus as your personal Savior, come see me any time—otherwise, I never want to see your faces around here again." Silently they left, I returned inside to my family, and we gave praise and thanks to God for sparing our lives that evening. I learned that night that if we resist Satan in the name of Jesus, he will flee. Satan is a big bully who turns into a coward when Jesus shows up (see James 4:7).

SIDE NOTE: Several years later I was in California taking some church training when I received a call from my secretary that a man in a local hospital was dying and had asked if I would come to him, saying he wanted to ask me for forgiveness. It turned out that he was one of the three men who had invaded our home and threatened our lives several years earlier, and now he was getting ready to meet God face to face and wanted to be forgiven for his demonic home invasion. I wanted so badly to make it home in time to pray with the man and assure him of God's mercy and forgiveness, but he passed into eternity before I could get there. I have confidence that God heard his plea and offered him pardon and salvation through Christ, the same one who defeated his demonic spirit on that Thursday-night home invasion.

The next several nights after the home invasion were filled with anxiety, and I admit also some fear for my family. Would they come back to finish Satan's job? I was certainly on edge particularly during the overnight hours. There's just something about the darkness, isn't there? Therefore, I put into action a popular plan for self-defense. It was called a twelve-gage shotgun. Please understand that I have never shot anyone and truthfully don't know that I could, but I did keep a loaded shotgun next to my bed at night just in case.

And then it happened. Three days later that same week, and in the middle of the darkest hours of night, I was awakened by the ringing of the doorbell, and I could feel the hair stand straight up on my head. That was the worst-case experience I ever had with what is called "the bed-head." I jumped up out of bed, and Darlene begged me not to answer the door. Of course, I had to answer it because I was the pastor and perhaps it was an emergency and someone needed my help. However, I did hand her the shotgun and advised her that if something happened to me, she had this gun to protect herself and the children. Darlene had not ever shot any kind of gun in her whole life, much less the twelve-gage shotgun that I used occasionally for rabbit hunting, and now I was asking her to defend herself and the kids from Satanic intruders who may be there to kill us! We lived too far from the city police to count on their getting there in time to save us. You can only try to imagine the fear that filled our home that night.

I made my way down the hallway, through the living room, to the front door and peered into the outside darkness through the little glass window in the door. I could see three silhouettes of unfamiliar men standing in the dark on the front porch. I whispered a quick prayer for our protection, turned on the porch light, opened the front door, and went outside, pulling the door closed behind me. I swallowed hard and asked with a trembling voice, "Can I help you?"

One of the three men stepped forward and asked, "Are you Rev. Walters?"

If there was ever a time I wanted to deny that I was me, this was the time. However, I answered "Yes, I am."

The man proceeded to tell me that he and his two buddies had just come from a Hamilton bar where they had been drinking all evening and into the night, and they knew they were lost sinners and had been told that I could help them find Jesus as their Savior. They were under the convicting power of the Holy Spirit.

Wow! My fear immediately turned into compassion and boldness for Christ. My knees quit shaking, my voice stopped trembling, and I invited them into my home. As my wife still sat in her bedroom holding the shotgun for protection, I sat at the kitchen table sharing salvation scriptures with three sinners who all gave their hearts to Jesus that night. What a slap in Satan's face! I recently officiated the funeral of one of those dear men, who is with the Lord in heaven today. Someday we'll meet again and talk about that night when out of the darkness came a light.

SPIRITUAL FORCES OF THIS DARK WORLD ARE AT WORK

Satan's schemes were manifested in many different ways, and often we could readily see them. Yet there was something more sinister going on within me that no one could see and I couldn't quite understand or explain. Satan unleashed a personal attack on me from his dark world unlike anything I had ever experienced. I mentioned earlier my driven desire to succeed and the terrible fear I had of failing. I would soon discover that it was motivated by the buried rejections that I had experienced as a teenager and as a young adult trying to answer the call of God for my life. Satan was drudging up all the pain that I thought was covered over years ago, and now it became so intense that it would lead me downward into a valley of depression and despair. He was reminding me that I would never succeed and that I would certainly fail and would never be free from the pain and hurts of the past rejections–I was trapped! I did not understand what was happening to me, nor was I able to explain it; therefore, it would become a depression of silence for some time yet to come.

Depression is defined as "feelings of severe despondency and dejection often caused by self-doubt and low self-image." Usually a depressed person feels very sad, hopeless, and unimportant and is often unable to live life in a normal way. That was becoming me–just ask my wife. She watched me change into a man she never knew: a man of seeming self-confidence, outgoing personality, and self-control to someone who turned inward and became angry and explosive over the smallest of things without warning or cause. Often this unexpected rage and anger were turned upon my wife and children. My marriage, my ministry, and even my life were being challenged by the buried rejections of the past that were beginning to emerge, and Satan was there to take every advantage of them. This was my condition while at the same time God was preparing us for the next stretch in our journey. I wondered—would this be the end for me?

To you who are reading this book, please listen: No matter how bad things are right now, no matter how stuck you feel, no matter how many days you've spent crying and wishing things were different, no matter how hopeless and depressed you are today, no matter how dark it is in your pit—I promise that you won't feel this way forever. Keep going. Don't quit. Help is on the way!

Mental pain is less dramatic than physical pain, but it is more common and also more difficult to bear. The frequent attempts to conceal mental pain often increases the burden. According to C. S Lewis in *The Problem of Pain,* it is easier to say, "My tooth is aching," than to say, "My heart is broken."

10

BE CAREFUL ABOUT WHAT YOU ASK FOR

Esau said to his father,
"Do you have only one blessing, my father?
Bless me too, my father!" Then Esau wept aloud
(Genesis 27:38)

Toward the end of summer 1985 I was returning from a Cincinnati hospital visit when I noticed at the intersection of Princeton Glendale Road and Tylersville Road a home mission Nazarene church. Their facilities consisted of a seventy-five-by-fifty-foot metal building that was used for worship, a small five-room shotgun-type farmhouse used as a parsonage, and an old barn that had been used during the farming days by the previous owner.

However, what really caught my attention was the thirty-two acres of land the little mission church sat on. I became envious and prayed the prayer of Esau in Genesis 27:38–"Do you have only one blessing, my father? Bless me too." I asked God to give my church in Hamilton the much-needed land as he had given that little home mission church so we could expand our facilities and continue to grow.

God heard my prayer, and only a few weeks later I received a call from the Southwestern Ohio Nazarene district superintendent–that's right, the same one whom God directed to call me to the little church in Hamilton–informing me that the small congregation of the home mission Nazarene church was asking if I would be willing to come and pastor their small congregation.

I was not interested in pastoring another congregation at this time. I was too involved in my own congregation in Hamilton, where God had placed me a few years earlier. However, the Lord directed me to see if they would be willing to sell us their land and facilities with the idea that we perhaps could relocate our Hamilton congregation to their location, contingent, of course, upon our church board approval. To my amazement the home mission church board agreed and gave me permission to approach my own church board with the proposition to sell their land and facilities with the condition that their home mission congregation would merge with our congregation. Wow–this thing was coming at me fast and hard! It was just a simple little prayer. What was I thinking? Was I crazy, or was God actually moving this way?

Knowing that our church sanctuary had reached its point of saturation in the Hamilton location and how we desperately needed to expand our facilities or face sure decline and how there was no more land on which to do so, I introduced the home mission board's proposition to our church board and told them that if they agreed, I would lead the way. However, the fear of failing began to rise up in me, so I presented my own contingencies to the deal called "green lights," another name for Gideon's fleeces.

I wrote down ten "green lights" or things that needed to happen, to try the Spirit and the will of the people to make sure this plan was of God. Admittedly, I was apprehensive about taking on such a monumental project, especially with my physical and emotional condition that was being spurred on by Satan's ongoing attacks, which were manifesting themselves in a whole new level of depression, pain, and fear of failure. I felt that if the congregation did not agree with these "green lights" it might be an honorable way out and I could save face by not failing at such a big project as relocation and the merger of two congregations.

I began listing the "green lights" by surveying the congregation to see where each person lived in relation to the new location. It turned out that fifty percent of them lived as close as to our church, twenty-five percent lived closer, and the other twenty-five percent lived a few miles farther away, and of those who lived farther away only a couple families supported the church with their tithes. These "green lights" would have to be approved by each of these categories of members for me to consider that it was God's will.

In the end, only about three families decided not to support the merger. Maybe this was a coincidence, so I decided to test God another way. Additional "green lights" involved the approval of a merger by the two local congregations and their church boards and by the Southwestern Ohio district superintendent and the district advisory board, as well as approval by the Nazarene denomination's Board of General Superintendents. If these four boards passed the proposition, it would have to be God!

Guess what! These "green lights" were passed by both congregations, and all four boards voted unanimously in favor of the proposition–and the merger was on. Plans were immediately put into action for the two congregations to merge as one, and I was to lead it!

Plans to combine the two congregations involved selling our Hamilton church facilities and parsonage and a small home used for church activities and relocate the congregation to the new location, twelve miles to the east of Hamilton. If you have ever tried to sell a church, a parsonage, and another small home together at the same time, you have an idea of the stress I was under. Couple that with the intensified battle of depression, anger, and pain that was going on inside me, and you could then possibly understand the fear of failure that gripped my soul. The responsibilities just got heavier. Could I really do all things through Christ, who gives me strength? We would soon find out.

While I was busy testing the waters with "green lights," God was busy working behind the scenes finding a buyer for our church. I was contacted by a realtor who represented a small church congregation who were interested in purchasing our church and parsonage. However, for personal reasons they had some contingencies of their own. We must take their small church building for a down payment, leave our classroom tables and chairs for them, and move out within twenty-four hours. What? Take it or leave it was the deal!

Realizing the difficulty of selling churches and the possibility that we might never get another offer, I called an emergency board meeting, and after serious discussion we signed the time-sensitive contract agreement. I put out a phone chain call to every church member and requested every abled-bodied man or woman and everyone with pickup trucks to meet at the church and parsonage at once for the quickest move in history. We were moving to our new location.

The church members responded to my call in big numbers with bodies and trucks and began removing all the church equipment and the parsonage furniture right down to the dresser drawers containing our personal unmentionables—this was not the time for etiquette—and within twelve hours we had vacated the church, the parsonage, and a small ministry home. This should have made national news or at least the *Guinness Book of World Records.*

Our new location's church facility was a fifty-by-seventy-five-foot metal multipurpose building that we used for worship. It was originally built to accommodate a small home mission congregation. An old barn sat on the property in front of the metal church building, and our new parsonage was a small evacuated farm house consisting of five small rooms and a bath. The thirty-two acres of land was surrounded by farms and cattle. It was a beautiful setting with room to grow. All the contents from the Hamilton location arrived at our new location, and whatever items we could not get into the multipurpose building and vacant parsonage we literally stashed inside the unused barn across the gravel driveway from the parsonage. It was a whirlwind of biblical proportions. A song from an old hymnal my father used to sing titled "When I Make My Last Move" became my favorite song and still is today.

In less than twenty-four hours we had moved from our old location to our new. Our family dwelling was downgraded from a beautiful, roomy brick ranch with three bedrooms, a living room, a dining room, a kitchen, two baths, and a partially finished basement to a barely livable narrow shotgun farm house with five small rooms, one bath, a wet basement, and an attic. I do believe God has a sense of humor. There–I said it!

That's not all! The cistern water in the parsonage was contaminated and not useable for drinking. However, we did reluctantly use it for showers before we investigated the cistern, only to discover that someone had thrown animals into it, live or dead we do not know. They had decomposed, leaving the water with a strange and unpleasant smell and taste. Let's not talk about that anymore. We did find another source of drinking water just up the road from our home–a natural underground spring that provided many residents with cool, clear tasty water. So we gathered one-gallon empty plastic milk cartons and hauled our drinking water from a natural spring water pipe located a on a country road approximately two miles west of our home.

Have you ever had the privilege of drinking natural spring water? We filled up approximately twenty one-gallon cartons at a time with good, free natural spring water. One day a man was there at the water trough looking at the spring water through a test tube. I asked him what he was doing there. He said he was a biochemist who worked for the county, which had been trying to shut the natural spring water trough down for many years but had not succeeded due to the outcry of the public to keep it open. He informed me that the spring water had been contaminated by vast amounts of cow dung that had filtered down through the ground from the surrounding cow pastures and seeped into the underground natural spring.

Then it hit me. We had been drinking spring water flavored with cow dung and standing in line for hours with other people to get our chance at the good stuff! Could this be the reason I caught my wife occasionally mooing like Bessy the heifer? Not funny! However, this was the only drinking water we had, so what could we do? Where there's a will there's always a way. The biochemist instructed me to fill each gallon carton with the spring water except for one inch from the top, then put two drops of bleach in each gallon carton of water and shake it vigorously, which would kill any bacteria, including that from cow dung. Hello! So we went from drinking water flavored with dead animals to drinking water flavored with cow dung–and now to now drinking water flavored with Clorox! I was thinking, *Am I living in America?* Some missionaries have it better than this! Just saying.

On November 14, 1985, the congregation met in the parking lot at the former church location and formed a parade of families with decorated cars and trucks. We were led by a sheriff escort as we made our way through the streets of Hamilton blowing our horns and waving goodbye to all we were leaving behind. We traveled twelve miles east across Tylersville Road to our new location at the corner of

Princeton Glendale Road. Upon our arrival the home mission congregation was waiting to graciously receive us into our newly merged church, and we all rejoiced and praised God for the great things He had done.

Finally the merger was completed—at least I thought so. I learned the hard way that merging two congregations does not necessarily mean assimilating them. No, merging and assimilation are definitely two different issues. The challenges became apparent almost immediately. Consider this: When our two churches merged, each was still individually incorporated and had separate bank accounts, which meant two separate offerings had to be received each Sunday and deposited into the appropriate accounts. Following the Nazarene *Manual* policy regarding elections of ministry directors and board members, we recognized that elections would not be held until May 1986, and this was only November 1985. Therefore, for the next six months I had to contend with two of everything: two directors of each ministry department, two Sunday School superintendents, and two missionary presidents. If that were not challenging enough, we had merged two church boards together consisting of twenty-six members. One half were white collar and the other half blue collar. What was I thinking? For your understanding, *blue collar* relates more to manual workers, particularly in industry. These make great followers for a pastor who can show them what to do to get the job done. White collar workers labor in an office or other professional environments and are more adapted to leading on their own. And now for the next six months I had to work with twenty-six men and women who had opposing attitudes toward leadership styles. At this point I wasn't even sure what my own leadership style was.

Thankfully the election day, when our church would elect new leaders, arrived in May 1986, and that presented me with another challenge: the prospect that the larger number of Hamilton church members would vote out all the smaller number of the home mission church members and thus create a schism within the two congregations. Thankfully, prayer and fasting prevailed again, and voting day went off without incident. At last we had one congregation, and we all agreed to call the two merged congregations the Tri-County Church of the Nazarene.

The complicated move took a big toll on my already-damaged health and emotions as I headed more deeply into the valley of depression. There were now even more ways to fail, and fear became an ugly two-headed monster in my mind. According to doctors, I suffered an emotional breakdown during this time and was going downhill fast. *Help me, God—I can't stop!*

THE TRAP OF SILENT DEPRESSION

1985 – THE MULTIPURPOSE BUILDING AND BARN

1985 – THE FIVE-ROOM FARMHOUSE PARSONAGE

11

THE MERGE, THE SUBMERGE, AND THE EMERGE

I appeal to you, brothers and sisters, in the name of our Lord Jesus Christ, that all of you agree with one another in what you say and that there be no divisions among you, but that you be perfectly united in mind and thought
(1 Corinthians 1:10)

My first pastoral experience immediately after the merger in November 1985 was dealing with a family who had lost their father and grandfather to a self-inflicted gunshot wound to the head. I rushed to the hospital trauma room where he lay barely conscious and prayed with him the sinner's prayer. He gave his heart to Jesus just minutes before he died.

Life gets hard for so many people just trying to survive from day to day, and despondency sometimes darkens our minds and robs us of hope. Many times such as this I was called upon to pray for someone whose need was critical. So was mine, but I kept quiet, trapped in silent depression.

The complicated move was not the only obstacle we faced in the merger. The small home mission multipurpose building was inadequate for Sunday morning worship services and the various church ministries. Therefore, we contracted a local high school space just down the road and began worshiping there on Sunday mornings. Each Sunday morning we would load up our song books, music instruments, a nine-by-twelve-foot roll of carpet to be used for the nursery, and take all this to the school for worship. After the worship service we would load it all up and bring it back to the small multipurpose building, where we had Sunday night service. It was a very difficult year and a half, particularly since at the same time we were breaking ground to build a new fourteen-thousand-square-foot sanctuary with class rooms. The strain and pressure of leading a major building program and conducting a capital building campaign only helped drive me more quickly to my emotional breaking point. That's another story for another book.

Regardless of how God had moved miraculously to bring the two congregations together, there were still some who decided that they did not like the merger, or for that matter me as their new pastor. Disgruntled and unhappy people have to be contended with immediately in order to keep the discontent from spreading to others. Therefore, I had to make many home visits to discuss the issues face to face in hopes of quelling the rising disunity. To my unpleasant surprise, I was often met with insults, hurtful words, and false accusations—and in one case I even had a door slammed in my face on a cold winter night. Satan never tired of using his tool of rejection on me. There I stood in the cold night, feeling foolish and needing a friend to rescue me from the carnal attacks being imposed upon me by good, unsuspecting people. It was a loneliness that I was becoming more accustomed to and just one of the many faces of depression.

Due to disunity, gossiping, and tale-bearing, coupled with the inability or unwillingness of some to assimilate with each other, an inevitable *sub-merge* was in the making, and the result would manifest itself in the loss of dozens of people in our first year together. It was a very discouraging time. Unity is a condition of harmony and oneness of mind, and when there is a crack in unity, division sets in and innocent people begin leaving. People come to church to worship, not to fight! Thankfully, the following year we attracted at least as many or more newcomers to the church to replace those who left us. I guess some would call that pruning in order to produce more fruit. Call it what you want, but we *emerged* in better shape and more unified than before.

In the midst of it all I suffered a serious physical breakdown during the first few months after the merger. In addition to depression and shaky emotions, my family and I had very little time or money to get away from the stress and demands of ministry for even a day, and it was taking its toll. Don't underestimate the emotional sufferings and emotional needs of pastors' spouses, who walk alongside their mates and endure their own unspoken pain in silence. A warning that my wife, Darlene, gives to church boards is as follows: "All work and no play, and no money and no vacations, make Jack a dull boy." Church boards must make sure the pastor and his or her spouse and family have some time away from the church and for each other. It does not have to be elaborate, but it must be intentional and timely. This is especially true for the pastor and family who live next door to the church. Some pastor's families prefer more privacy than the parsonage provides, especially true of the small church. They often become the unofficial custodian of the church, having to provide access to anyone needing entrance to the church facilities, from a repairman, to a visitor. Too often they must be the one who unlocks and closes the facilities for the various activities, including taking responsibilities for lights, heat and air settings. The list is endless, and add to all this, the increased stress of their constantly being under the critical observation of the entire congregation.

I remember vividly our last scheduled vacation just before the merger. My wife and I secured someone to watch our children while we took a few days away. We were so excited, and I had built up in my mind the perfect vacation. I was dealing with severe depression, and to go anywhere, any place, just to change the environment would perhaps bring a sense of relief from the pain my wife and I were experiencing. Finally the day came, and we were off, with our first stop planned for Memphis. We drove over seven hours to our destination before pulling into the motel where we had secured reservations. We grabbed our suitcases from the trunk of the car and headed to the office to check in.

The kind lady at the counter asked, "Are you Rev. Walters?"

I replied "Yes, I am."

She said, "There's a phone message waiting for you in your room." This, of course, was before the days of cell phones. So I retrieved the message from the phone in our room, which simply said, "Pastor, come home quickly. My husband is going to have emergency heart surgery at 8:00 in the morning, and he's asking for you. We're not sure he'll make it through."

We immediately picked up our unpacked suit cases, put them back into the trunk of the car, and I drove all night long in silence while my wife quietly cried the whole way back home. I did get back in time for the emergency heart surgery that morning. I rushed down to the hospital with an exhausted body and swollen eyes from no sleep–to find the kind, elderly man who was going to have surgery sitting up in his room in a recliner reading his newspaper and drinking coffee.

I stood there in shock and disbelief as he said, "Pastor, didn't they get in touch with you? My surgery has been canceled!" Satan laughed at me, and I immediately descended several rungs lower on the ladder of depression. My wife and I were very despondent–our time and much of our meager vacation budget were depleted, so we simply went back to work.

A pastor friend of mine told me that he developed a rule of thumb for hospital emergency visitation that I might want to consider. He says to his congregation, "If you call me at 2:30 in the morning and get me out of bed and tell me to come quickly, that someone is dying–when I get there the person had better die!" He was just joking– I think.

The parsonage, if located next to the church, must be a place of solitude and privacy for the pastor and his family. People would often walk into our parsonage totally unannounced and literally take ownership of our personal food items such as sugar and cream, for church functions and classroom coffee, or they would bring their kids in to play with our children's toys. One mother told her kid when he broke one of our children's favorite toys not to worry about it since "it belonged to the church anyhow." One of our little boys came crying to his mother asking her if it was true that all his toys belonged to the church. Some children have grown up and left church for less than that.

If the female church members could simply visualize living within eyesight of their husband's place of employment and having his coworkers drop in on them unannounced every day to borrow salt and sugar for the coffee room at their place of employment and stop in unannounced with their children to play with your kids' toys–they could soon grasp what it is like to be a pastor's wife and live in a parsonage. Some pastors and pastor's wives resent, and rightfully so, living in a fish bowl. If you are into fish, go watch the movie *Finding Nemo*–just saying.

One day my wife and kids were away from the parsonage, and I took advantage of the situation to relax. Now, relaxing to me meant being alone in a quiet room, in total privacy, lying back in my recliner clothed only in my Fruit of the Looms. That's right–preachers wear Fruit of the Looms too! It took only a few minutes for me to fall into la-la land. So there you have it. I was having sweet dreams in the middle of the afternoon when a lady friend of my wife from the church entered unannounced through our kitchen door, and I was unaware that my wife, who left in a hurry, had mistakenly left the kitchen door unlocked. Calling for my wife, her lady friend made her way through the dining room into the living room, where I sat sound asleep wearing only my unmentionables. I was awakened by a blood-curdling scream, the kind you hear when someone sees Freddy Kruger heading toward him or her with a chain saw, and when I saw her I screamed back as loud as I could. And there we were, face to face screaming at each other at the top of our voices. She tried to apologize for invading my privacy as she literally ran back through the dining room into the kitchen and out the back door. You can believe we didn't make eye contact again for a long time, but neither did she ever again walk into our house unannounced.

THE TRAP

*L*ORD*, hear my prayer, listen to my cry for mercy; in your faithfulness and righteousness come to my relief* (Psalm 143:1).

My emotional breakdown was a precursor to my deepest depression to date and threatened to derail my entire ministry. The days of coping with my unstable feelings were becoming unbearable. I reached out to my family doctor for help, and he began treating me medically for depression in the winter of 1985. He also recognized that I was experiencing suicidal tendencies and recommended that I get out of the pressures of ministry in order to save myself. He also threatened to call my church board and tell them of the seriousness of my condition if I did not make them aware. He insisted that I go into a hospital for a couple of weeks so I could be observed, or at the very least take a couple weeks away from the church ministry to be in solitude. I felt embarrassed and ashamed. This is the stigma that goes along with depression.

Feeling trapped in my silent depression, I could not tell it to the church board or to the congregation for fear that they would panic because now they had a sick pastor on their hands. I could not tell it the district superintendent, whose responsibility it was to make sure that the pastor has the wellness and ability to oversee and manage the church, and I did not want to be put on the "black list" of sick pastors.

Coupled with this driven desire to succeed and a result of past rejections, the walls of failure were now seemingly closing in on me. I began thinking that if there were only an honorable way out, I would take it—and death begin looking more and more appealing if it could just bring an end to my pain without imposing disgrace upon my wife and children. These thoughts at times became foremost in my mind.

Many Sunday mornings I would sit in my office before the worship service just staring into space and unable to go out to greet the congregation. My wife would come in and say, "Honey, they're waiting on you," and I would say, "I can't go out there today." She would then pray for me, help me to my feet, and give me the courage to proceed to the platform. I would put on my forced smile, greet the people, and the service would begin. The merciful Spirit of the

Lord would come upon me and give me unction to preach, and when the service was over I would go back to my office and often collapse in my chair or on the floor until I could bring myself to get up to go home and get under the covers and stay there all afternoon.

By now most mornings at home were being spent in a dark bedroom under the covers with the curtains pulled closed. I felt I could not face another day. I was trapped in my depression, and no one knew except for my wife, who had to suffer the consequences of my depression's silent trap. *Silent* depression is the worst kind of all. Who can I tell? Who would understand? Will I survive? Who will take care of my family? Will God forgive me? *Help me, God–I can't go on!*

In the earlier stage of my depression and before the merger of the two congregations, my wife describes me as having experienced between two and four emotionally explosive episodes per week over anything or nothing at all. Example: Getting bad food or service at a restaurant became a big deal when normally it would not have been a problem at all. But after the merger the episodes of emotional explosions came more regularly without warning and never knowing what would trigger them. In the heat of the outbursts I would usually lay the blame on my wife and kids, and they would receive the wrath of my rage and cruel words. It's true–the human, carnal tendency is to hurt the ones we love the most and are closest to. After all, it's their love for us that garners the attention we most want and need when no one else understands us and when we don't understand ourselves.

I would later cry, try to make up, and say I just couldn't help myself. My self-esteem only sank lower into the pit of shame and despair. My wife and children walked on their tiptoes trying to stay out of my way so as to not trigger something that would set off my anger. The thing I feared most was happening—I was failing, not just as a pastor but also as a husband and father and as a man of God.

While writing this book I asked my wife, Darlene, who has been my faithful helpmate in ministry and who suffered with me during this dark time of our lives, to tell me how it affected her. How did she view me during this time as a Christian and as a pastor? Did she feel her insecurity slipping away? I was having these explosions that I could not account for while simultaneously trying to do ministry—it was an oxymoron. Many times I felt unworthy to stand behind the pulpit and handle the Word of God. I wondered if she viewed me as being real or as a phony. Often I could not distinguish the difference myself. It was difficult for me to tell whether the explosions were a result of my physical sickness, my spiritual sickness, or both. Mental actions and mean action are often difficult to differentiate. However, when actions are a result of mental-physical sickness, coupled with spiritual carnal meaness, it becomes a mixture of mental-ness and mean-ness. Therefore, I call it mean-tal-ness. One is helped by medicine and the other by repentance.

Darlene's answer was that she always knew I was sincere and real and that the way I was acting was because I was very sick. She also felt I had experienced a personality change due to medicines, one of which caused me to hallucinate during my sleep and another robbing me of my humor—the laughs and smiles were all gone. At the lowest point of my depression she felt her normal life as she had known it was over, that we would live the duration of our lives this way, and that because of my physical condition I would not live long. She was concerned that in my rages I would have a heart attack, a stroke, or even worse. The doctor agreed that due to the number of physical problems I was experiencing, coupled with the serious suicidal tendencies and the silent depression that could not be exposed or shared for various reasons, my future in ministry was being seriously threatened unless there was a drastic change in my life. My wife, of course, was trapped also.

A SIDE NOTE: Some personalities are more susceptible to depression than others. Therefore, it is a great benefit to understand the different personality types and characteristics of each one. My personality type (melancholy) has many characteristics that aided my depression in a very negative way. While people of all personality types may experience depression, some are more unforgiving, resentful, insecure, pessimistic, extra-sensitive, skeptical, critical, and revengeful. Unfortunately, I did not have this important information before or during my state of depression. I learned afterwards that many people suffer depression and remain there longer due to their lack of understanding the negative characteristics of their personalities.

I would highly recommend a personality profile specially designed for individual understanding called Personality Plus, by Florence Littauer. It may be ordered from

> CLASS
> P. O. Box 66810
> Albuquerque, NM 87193
> at 800-433-6633, or www.classervices.com.

12

HELP ME, LORD—I'M FALLING

You have put me in the lowest pit,
in the darkest depths
(Psalm 88:6)

I HAD RUNNING ON MY MIND

Heading into the spring of 1987, I was at my lowest point in depression. I had learned to wear a smile for the sake of my survival and to keep from admitting that I was failing. Yet at the same time I experienced an indescribable pain and hurt on the inside and was looking for a way out of my inward prison. Many times, usually on Monday mornings after a difficult Sunday service, I would sit down to write my resignation letter or to phone the district superintendent to tender my resignation, only to forget the letter or to hang up the phone before he had a chance to answer. Many times I wanted to run as far as I could, just to get away from it all and even die there.

I related to Elijah's victorious battle on Mount Carmel (1 Kings 18) that turned into the biggest nightmare of his life overnight (1 Kings 19). He was bold enough on the mountaintop to stand up to 850 false prophets, yet only hours later in the valley he could not face up to one cruel woman who threatened to end his life by the next day. So he ran for his life, and eventually, exhausted, weary, and fearful, he ended up inside a cave at Mount Horeb–the same mountain where God gave the Ten Commandments to Moses. God knew where Elijah was hiding and came to the entrance of the cave, whispering gently, *Elijah, what are you doing here?*

This is the same emotional roller coaster I was on–bold one day and fear-driven the next. And now at my lowest and darkest depth of depression, I actually had running on my mind! My inability to cope was now becoming my inability to hope. Hearing about a pastor friend who had been hospitalized in Knoxville, Tennessee, I began thinking that this was my chance to run, my excuse to get out of town, out of my misery, out of my pain. I made plans to get into my car and head to Knoxville, visit my friend in the hospital, get back into my car, and just keep heading south or west to anywhere or nowhere–maybe even to Mt. Horeb, where I could find a cave to hide in. But God would always show up in the nick of time to make a way for me to escape when these terrible temptations would come.

No temptation has overtaken you except what is common to mankind. And God is faithful; he will not let you be tempted beyond what you can bear. But when you are tempted, he will also provide a way out so that you can endure it (1 Corinthians 10:13).

Only an hour or so before time came for me to proceed with my plan to run, I got a call from the district superintendent. He was always showing up in God's behalf just in time. The Lord used this man to keep an eye on me. My district superintendent knew something wasn't right about me and asked if he could come visit for a while. When I told him I was leaving town to visit a pastor friend hospitalized in Knoxville, he asked if he could ride along with me so we both could visit him and we could chat along the way. What could I say? God was intervening, and the devil's scheme was foiled again!

On our way to Knoxville he shared that God had impressed upon him to come and be with me this day and to encourage me in the Lord. We visited the pastor in Knoxville and returned home. On the way back, I opened up and shared my worsening depression and feelings. He had compassion on me and prayed with me. It was a great relief to know that now that the cat was out of the bag and that at least I had a friend who would listen to my cry and empathize with my sickness. God's eye really is upon the sparrow, and now I was assured that He was watching me.

SEARCHING FOR ANSWERS

So many times I recommended people to seek out counseling with a Christian psychologist. One man humorously said, "Anyone who goes to a psychologist should have his head examined." However, I took my own advice and tried counseling with one. My medicine was failing me. I could not see an end to the darkness and just needed someone to unload on, someone who could help relieve my pain. But the $70 an hour, money that I did not have, only produced more guilt in me by taking money from my family, who needed it so badly for other things. My life had descended into a viscous cycle of darkness, fear, and pain with no end in sight, and the darkness had become so great that often in the middle of a sunny, cloudless day I would sit next to a bright lamp in an effort to dispel the darkness. I was trapped in my depression.

I eventually made an appointment with a Christian counselor. He was kind and understanding, so we sat down together and I began sharing my depression story with him. He listened to me intently, and then to my surprise within a few moments he began sharing his own depression story with me. You see, depression is no respecter of a person's age, gender, or social status. And wouldn't you know it? We both sat there together in his office crying and praying for each other. It was a helpful time for both of us. However, a few days later I received a bill for $70. I felt that he should have at least shared half of the bill. Some have asked, "How many psychologists does it take to change a light bulb?" Answer: "Just one–but it takes nine visits." Remember what I said earlier–God really does have a sense of humor.

The kind psychologist really did help me identify some things in my past that were triggering my depression, things that had been blocked out of my mind for years and lay buried deep beneath the surface from a long time ago, particularly the concealed rejections that I had experienced as a young man. He instructed me to sit down and write out in longhand every hurtful memory beginning as far back as I could remember. Willing to try anything to relieve the inward pain, I sat down at home and begin writing on a yellow legal pad every hurtful memory from childhood up to the present.

ARE YOU A BOY OR ARE YOU A GIRL?

I began writing my life's story by longhand, and as I tried to recollect the hurtful memories from my childhood, youth, and young adult years, unstoppable tears began flowing. Let's get one thing straight–who is there among us who cannot go back and drudge up something unpleasant from our childhood? I remember a young man telling me one time with a serious face that he could remember his mother sticking him with a diaper pin right after he was born, and he felt she did it on purpose. Now he was a grown man and was still suffering from that hurtful experience, real or perceived.

I don't have any experiences like that in my childhood. I had the privilege being one of seven children with hardworking and sincere, loving parents who left us a Christian heritage that we treasure and pass on to our children and grandchildren even today. However, every once in a while I pull out the one and only baby picture of me, taken when I was a few months old—a two-by-three-inch black-and-white that has survived many decades. My family and I have a big laugh every time we look at it. There I am, a pitiful little specimen wearing nothing but a smile and a dress. A dress? That's right—a dress! At least it looks like one, even though my mother assured me that it was a little gown that was common for boy babies in the 1940s. Nevertheless, each time the family views the picture they laugh and sing the song recorded in 1965 by the Barbarians, "Are You a Boy or Are You a Girl?" Even the name on my birth certificate was misspelled by an in-home delivery doctor who listed my name as Danee' instead of Danny. Go figure.

I can remember the spankings and the threats as a child all the way through pre-adolescence, including the time-honored threat "I'm going to tell your father when he gets home." That was the very last thing I wanted to hear. And Mom and Dad did assign chores to us, such as hoeing the weeds in the garden and watering the garden plants that we would harvest in the fall so we could can and preserve them for the winter's food supply. Today this would be called child abuse! But now that Mom and Dad are with Jesus, I find myself praising them for the fine job they did raising seven children with less than an eighth-grade education. Were they successful parents? You'd better believe it—all seven children came to know Christ Jesus as personal Savior. And who do I want to see first when I get to heaven? Jesus, of course. And who do I want to see next? You got it—Mom and Dad. I made it through my childhood unharmed, unscarred, and dearly loved. Let's move on.

As I continued writing, I was learning quickly through this written exercise that the anger I had been suppressing and ignoring much of my life was beginning to surface. I also discovered that whenever we ignore or bury an emotion, it is buried alive—and that at some point and in some way the ignored or buried emotion will rise up and express itself physically, psychologically, or spiritually. In my case it was all three.

One of my sons asked me one day after one of my anger explosions, "Dad, why are you always so happy at church and so angry at home?" It broke my heart to see what I was doing to my children and wife. Unable to understand it myself, I brushed it aside.

One of the primary emotions, such as fear and sadness, can be found underneath buried anger. Feeling fear and sadness is uncomfortable, and it makes you feel vulnerable and often not in control. I guess this is why people tend to avoid these feelings any way they can, even keeping them buried where no one can see them even though they're very much alive. They simply become part of the trap of silent depression.

I believe most of us experience the issue of anger and react emotionally to distressing situations. Common roots of anger include fear, pain, and frustration. For example, some people become angry as a fearful reaction to uncertainty. Others become angry because of the fear of losing a job or the fear of failure. Still others become angry when they are hurt in relationships or are caused pain by a close friend. In my case the root of anger was found in the pain of rejection by my significant others. The pain of rejection is one of the strongest negative factors in a person's life, especially in a younger person who finds security and trust in the persons he or she has looked up to, whether it be a parent, a relative, a friend, a teacher, a pastor, or some other significant person. Once rejected by these trusted individuals, the person finds the walls of self-confidence and security falling down all around him or her, replaced with insecurity, a low self-image, a fear of failing, and a need for approval. The end result is pain and often bitterness toward the one who has dealt the blow of rejection, disloyalty, or betrayal.

The American Psychological Association defines *anger* as "an emotion characterized by antagonism toward someone you feel has deliberately done you wrong." However, anger can also be a good thing. It can give you a way to express negative feelings or motivate you to find solutions to problems. For me anger was a good thing in that it motivated me to succeed over my fear of failure, and I was determined to succeed at any cost, to show anyone and everyone, especially those who had rejected me, that I was not a failure–and anger for me in the positive sense became one of my drivers for the "Big MO." The "Big Mo' is a church growth term describing a behavioral momentum that has a positive effect of an individual's performance.

THE WONDER YEARS

A common definition of *wonder* is "to be filled with admiration, amazement, or awe; to marvel." My teen years were totally consumed by one object of my affection (other than God)–her name was Darlene Kay Aishe. I was fourteen years old, and she was the most beautiful little twelve-year-old girl I had ever laid my eyes on. There she stood on the platform of our home church in Cincinnati singing for Jesus with big hazel eyes, curly auburn hair, and a voice like an angel. I was hit square in the heart by God's love arrow.

This was the beginning of my wonder years of admiration, amazement, and awe for the love of my life that God would mold together as one to bring glory to himself for decades to come.

Most testimonies are developed from the painful experiences in our lives. How often I have drawn from the pain I have endured in my own life so that others could see God working through the pain in their lives! I'll never forget the painful experience of my wife's mother passing away at age forty-nine of a sudden heart attack. I was hospitalized and unable to be with her, and at only seventeen she had to face her mother's death and funeral alone without me. Then following the funeral she had to deal with the painful experience of her father contemplating sending her away to another state to live with relatives, thus breaking up our six-year love affair. Our hearts were broken at the thought and resulted in our eloping at ages seventeen and nineteen. We didn't have a big wedding or honeymoon, but we had each other, and that was enough to keep us going.

We returned home to Cincinnati from a two-day elopement trip to Winchester, Kentucky, and I stopped at a phone booth in Cincinnati to call my dad to let him know we were back. However, I was so nervous from the elopement that I dialed Darlene's father by mistake. He answered, and thinking he was my own father, I called him "Daddy." It was just a little too soon for that and certainly got us started off on the wrong foot. We drove on over to her father's house, and he met us in the driveway, very angry. As a businessman, his first question was "Do you have insurance on my daughter?"

And I, being a young *un*-businessman, could think of no other insurance but car insurance, so I answered, "Yes, I have liability." The situation went downhill from there. It would be five years before he would speak to me. I was rejected again!

The ultimate hurt I experienced as a teenager was that of rejection. Rejection is the spurning or distain of a person's affections, and I always had a fondness for preaching. Even as a five-year-old child, I remember my two older brothers and sister and me playing church in our home in Newtown, Ohio. We would sing, I would pretend to preach, and they would respond by coming to a makeshift altar to pray. Fast-forward to age eleven. I remember standing in front of a big dresser mirror in Mom and Dad's bedroom and preaching so hard and fast that I preached myself under conviction and fell down on my knees on the floor to pray. Now that's good preaching—when you can get yourself to your own altar!

Even during my teen years the church was my life, and now my wife and I were a young married couple, seventeen and nineteen, who loved God and loved singing for the Lord. Therefore, it was only logical that God, who put us together as children and worked in us through the wonder years of our lives, was now preparing us for something greater than ever before. His hand had been on our lives since we were born. Now as a teen, I heard God calling me!

I continued writing, and it took me back to my call to ministry at age nineteen and the unseemly rejection by my significant others, which I explained in chapter one. The more I wrote the more I sobbed, and the more I sobbed the more I drugged up the hurt and pain that I had buried deep in my sub-consciousness as a nineteen-year-old young man, and it was still very much alive! This exercise of writing out my life's story was very helpful in that it made me aware that my depression was in great part a consequence of buried rejection. I had filled out a whole legal pad of tear-stained pages, and then I took them to the Lord, prayed over them, and burned them, letting the smoke rise up before his nostrils as incense. David prayed in Psalm 141:2, "May my prayer be set before you like incense."

The altar of incense can be seen as a symbol of the prayers of God's people. Our prayers ascend to God as the smoke of the incense ascended in the sanctuary. That day God smelled the incense of my prayers for mercy and deliverance from the trap of silent depression, and the long nights of darkness would soon come to an end. Little did I know—*the answer was on the way!*

13

CARRIED AWAY IN THE SPIRIT

Weeping may stay for a night,
but rejoicing comes in the morning
(Psalm 30:5)

From 1981 until 1987 I literally fought a spiritual battle against Satan and his demons, and for three years, from 1984 to 1987, I fought the greatest battle of my life against my own personal trap of silent depression. Yet in the midst of it all, these were some of the best days of my ministry. God has always been able to work in spite of our own shortcomings. However, the challenges of growing a church while raising a family and the unrelenting demands of pastoring were beginning to take their toll on me. The overwhelming challenge came when Satan began to drudge up the hurt and pain that I thought had been buried a long time ago but now were raising their ugly heads from their temporary grave and were very much alive.

In 1987 a district pastor's conference was conducted at one of the neighboring Nazarene churches. Most pastors' meetings are usually very reserved and quiet, and so it was that day in 1987. Someone said you can tell a preacher a long way off, but the closer they get you can't tell him or her anything. That could be true for a lot of us. At any rate, there my wife and I sat in the sanctuary waiting for the service to begin. A good crowd of pastors and wives were there that day sitting quietly and reserved as good Nazarenes do. I often joked about Nazarenes being the first to rise in the rapture since the Bible says in 1 Thessalonians 4:16, "The dead in Christ will rise first."

The service was preceded by the normal district announcements and a chiding of pastors who did not get their monthly statistics reported to the district office on time. We also were scolded for our lack of participation in the recent denominational *Herald of Holiness* campaign. Once again I wanted to say "Well, bless God– tell me more." This triggered my already negative attitude, and all I wanted was to just get out of there, go home, and cover my head. However, my wife encouraged me to stay. Pastor's spouses have a way of doing that. What would pastors do without the encouragement of their spouses?

We had a guest evangelist speak to us about some of the great revivals of past centuries. He preached about the call of God upon the lives of some of the great men and women of God in years gone by. It was somewhere at this point that God spoke to me about my own call to ministry. A panorama instantly passed before my eyes and reminded me of my call at age nineteen when I was carried away in the Spirit to the very entrance of hell and God fought Satan, winning the battle for my soul; and again at age thirty-one when he rekindled the fire that raged within my bones.

And then it happened–the power of the Holy Spirit began moving in my heart and over my body and physically lifted me up from my seat in the middle of the sanctuary and stood me on my feet. The power of God was so strong that it moved me out across the row of people, into the center isle of the church, down to the front of the sanctuary, and threw me onto my face at the altar. Once again I was carried away in the Spirit and lay there on the floor, being ministered to by the healing hands of Jesus himself. Once again He was fighting the enemy of my soul, my body, and my mind. Satan was defeated once and for all that day, and the trap door to my silent depression sprang open wide. It was dispelled for good, along with the pain of rejection and the fear of failing.

I was free. No longer would I have to keep silent for fear of what others would think or do. No longer would I have to hide in a dark room with the curtains pulled closed with covers over my head because I couldn't face the day. No longer would I have to wear a fake smile or mistreat my wife and kids. No longer would the binds of rejection hold me prisoner. I walked out of my own prison that day a free man!

My wife, along with many others present that day, described the scene for me. Those quiet and reserved pastors all over the church stood simultaneously with raised hands toward heaven and with shouts and praises. Some walked and some literally ran around the sanctuary as the Shekinah glory fell upon the people. No one knew exactly what was happening up front with Dan Walters, but one thing they all knew for certain was that Jesus had walked in and was doing business with the devil!

Pastors came forward and literally surrounded me at the altar, the district superintendent leading the way. They prayed for twenty minutes or more, and when I regained consciousness I heard the prayers and weeping of my fellow pastors getting louder and louder, and the lights in the sanctuary getting brighter and brighter. I sat up on the floor and proclaimed to all around me, "It's gone. It's gone."

"What is gone?" the district superintendent asked.

I cried out loud, "The darkness, the pain, the fear–it's gone. It's all gone!"

The darkness and depression had been driven out and expelled. The unrelenting pain that had tormented me for the past three years had lost its grip and control. Satan was defeated–he had to flee. I wrote a song that describes what happened that day. In part in goes like this: "Satan walked out when Jesus walked in. / The power of His blood has cleansed every sin. / Satan thought he had me for good, / But then Satan walked out when Jesus walked in!"

It was Jesus who–

Healed the mother of Peter's wife.

Healed the deaf-mute of Decapolis.

Healed the blind at birth.

Healed the paralytic at Bethesda.

Healed blind Bartimaeus in Jericho.

Healed the centurion's servant.

Healed an infirm woman.

He added me to the list. The Lord healed me from the sickness of depression and opened the trap door to my dark prison where I was held hostage, and just like Lazarus in John 11, who had been dead four days, Jesus raised me from my physical and emotional deadness and made me alive again!

The first words that came to my mind and that I spoke with my mouth were "I have sinned." The Holy Spirit revealed to me that somewhere along the journey of darkness I had neglected my prayer life and had begun focusing on the darkness instead of the light. My faith in God's ability to heal became weak, and I had given the devil a foothold in my heart by allowing the sun to go down on my wrath and by sinning in my anger (see Ephesians 4:26-27). I repented and prayed for forgiveness, and God restored the joy of my salvation. He performed a healing miracle in me that day and gave me a fresh new start! I was healed from my trap of silent depression by the power and authority of Jesus Christ, and my sins were washed white as snow by the precious blood of the Lamb! (Revelation 12:11).

Many of you reading this book are being held hostage in your own trap of silent depression. You feel alone, rejected, or even betrayed. You feel that no one understands. I want you to know today that God understands, He knows all about it, and He hears your silent plea for deliverance. Perhaps you harbor unforgiven sins in your heart, you have abandoned your prayer life, or your faith has been weakened in God's ability to perform a miracle in you. Perhaps you have given up on deliverance, and Satan has convinced you that there is no hope. Cry out to God right now in repentance and faith, and ask Him to carry you away in the Spirit and fight Satan for your soul. Ask Him to add you to the list of the redeemed and the healed.

The righteous cry out, and the LORD hears them; he delivers them from all their troubles. The LORD is close to the brokenhearted and saves those who are crushed in spirit (Psalm 34:17-18).

CONCLUSION

Give thanks in all circumstances;
for this is God's will for you in Christ Jesus
(1 Thessalonians 5:18)

Notice that 1 Thessalonians 5:18 says to give thanks *in* all circumstances–it does not say *for* all circumstances. Thankfulness makes the enemy flee. The forces of darkness can't stand being around hearts that give thanks and honor to God. Our praise and thanksgiving in all things will make evil forces flee. God loves to give good gifts to His children. He delights in our thankfulness and pours out His Spirit and favor over those who give honor and gratitude to Him, those who desire that He work all things out for their good. Yes, even the dark valley of depression can be used for His good (see Romans 8:28).

So many times I pick up the phone only to hear someone weeping on the other end, saying something like "Someone told me that you've battled depression, and I just wondered if you would be willing to talk with me about mine." I always say, "Sure I will." Because I have traveled in that valley, I know how to relate. God has used my own depression to give hope to many others who are being enslaved by it. Therefore, I give thanks *in* all circumstances, even depression, that it may be used for the glory of God.

The next several months after my healing I was especially aware when waking up in the morning that the lights were on, the curtains were open, and the sun was shining brightly, even on cloudy days. I'm always aware that even when the clouds are hanging low and hide the sun from my view–it's still up there. It's the same with our heavenly Father. I would always begin my day by saying, "Thank You, Lord, that I'm not depressed today." One day God spoke sweetly to me and said, *Don't fear, My son. You don't have to thank Me every day–just enjoy your new freedom and healing. I love you.*

That was thirty years ago, and today I can look back to the sacred spot where Jesus said, "It's enough." He knew my breaking point and promised a way to escape it (1 Corinthians 10:13). Along with the casting-out of depression went the pain of rejection, feelings of low self-esteem, the fear of failure, and the unhealthy motivation to succeed that was driven by anger. Ministry became "others"-centered and Kingdom-focused. The church began to thrive, ministry became rewarding, and my wife and children could see the difference in me. They were also set free! I was free to be myself, free from the moods of intense sadness and evil thoughts, free from negative thinking, and free to succeed for God. No longer did I want to run away *from* God– now I wanted to run *to* God!

Today many pastors and lay people are experiencing the same trap of rejection and depression that I was in and perhaps are suffering in silence. This may be you, and you can't explain it–you just know it hurts. Maybe your circumstances or situations and experiences are different than mine, but you know the feelings of low self-esteem and lack of self-confidence that come from rejection or betrayal by your significant others or from being beaten down by some in your congregation and possibly even by your spouse. Perhaps your fear of failing is intensified by your previous failures and it's been a long time since you've had a win under your belt. Perhaps you have thoughts of returning to the secular workforce–anything to relieve your pain and frustration so you won't have to face failure again.

There is hope! Just like Joseph, who was rejected by his brothers, stripped of his coat of many colors, and thrown into a dark pit, he looked up and saw a caravan coming. Look up today–a caravan is coming for *you*!

Many pastors today are tempted to step out of the light rather than stay in the light and fight for the cause that God has called them to. I want you to know that God is not through performing miracles—I am a witness! At the end of my resources, I was broken and helpless, so weakened that I could not go to Him any longer—but He came to me as He did to Elijah, who was hiding in a dark cave on Mount Horeb fearing the wrath of Jezebel. First Kings 19:11-13 records the story:

> The Lord said, "Go out and stand on the mountain in the presence of the Lord, for the Lord is about to pass by." Then a great and powerful wind tore the mountains apart and shattered the rocks before the Lord, but the Lord was not in the wind. After the wind there was an earthquake, but the Lord was not in the earthquake. After the earthquake came a fire, but the Lord was not in the fire. And after the fire came a gentle whisper. When Elijah heard it, he pulled his cloak over his face and went out and stood at the mouth of the cave. Then a voice said to him, "What are you doing here, Elijah?"

Perhaps you can hear the Lord whispering to you right now, *Come out of your cave—what are you doing here? Bring your rejections, your fears, your broken self-confidence, and your dark depression to Me.*

Ask God to do for you what He did for me thirty years ago at a small church altar. Make an altar right where you are and fall on your knees, for it is no secret what God can do–what he did for Elijah on Mount Horeb he can do for you in your valley today. The coming of Jesus was for people like you and me. He said in Luke 4:18, "He has sent me to proclaim freedom for the prisoners . . . to set the oppressed free." Claim His promise today. He wants to free you from your trap of silent depression.

PRAY PSALM 3:1-8

Lord, how many are my foes!
> How many rise up against me!

Many are saying of me,
> "God will not deliver him."

But you, Lord, are a shield around me,
> my glory, the One who lifts my head high.

I call out to the Lord,
> and he answers me from his holy mountain.

I lie down and sleep;
> I wake again, because the Lord sustains me.

I will not fear though tens of thousands
> assail me on every side.

Arise, Lord!
> Deliver me, my God!

Strike all my enemies on the jaw;
>   break the teeth of the wicked.
From the Lord comes deliverance.
>   May your blessing be on your people.
Amen.

APPENDIX
Additional Stories

AN UNFORGETTABLE VISIT

You also must be ready, because the Son of Man will come at an hour when you do not expect him (Matthew 24:44)

One of the first responsibilities of a pastor's new assignment is to start calling on those on the church enrollment list. On one of my very first visits I made my way up the walkway onto the porch of a humble community home. I heard the television set blaring on the inside, so I knocked on the door and waited patiently for someone to answer. Finally a young, full-figured lady answered the door wearing a very skimpy two-piece swim suit, which reminded me of Bobby Darin's 1959 hit song "Itsy Bitsy Teenie Weenie Yellow Polkadot Bikini." In a rough voice she asked, "What do you want?"

I replied, "I'm the new pastor of your church, and I just stopped by to introduce myself to you and invite you to church this Sunday."

She let out with a scream, and hollered, "Oh, my God!"

I replied, "No, I'm not God, but He's coming unannounced just like this one day."

She ran and grabbed pillows from the couch to hide her nakedness, but they were insufficient. Then she ran into the dining room and in one motion jerked the table spread from the dining room table, wrapped it around her exposed body, and said, "Pastor, would you like to come in?"

"No," I replied. "I just want to invite you out for Sunday service, and I hope to see you there." I left her standing at her front door with a table spread wrapped carefully around her body. God and I had a chuckle together that day. Neither one of us will ever forget that visit!

THE DAY I ALMOST WON THE LOTTERY

Those who trust in their riches will fall,
but the righteous will thrive like a green leaf
(Proverbs 11:28)

I was so excited when a lady telephoned me one day to request that I pray for her and her family. She said, "Pastor, please pray—we have a chance to win a Publishers Clearing House prize of nine million dollars." Wow! I began dreaming and putting some figures together in my head—a tithe on nine million dollars would be $900,000. Our problems would be solved: a new sanctuary, an educational facility, a gymnasium with showers and more, a raise for the pastor! Then my dreams were abruptly interrupted by the lady when she said, "Pastor, my family has already talked it over, and we've agreed that if we win the nine million, we're going to give the church one thousand dollars." There went my dreams. One thousand dollars was $899,000 dollars less than I was thinking about—and there goes my raise too!

TWO LOUISVILLE SLUGGERS AND GOD

*The name of the Lord is a fortified tower;
the righteous run to it and are safe
(Proverbs 18:10)*

Our parsonage was a small farm house with an attached solarium—a room with extensive windows to allow plenty of sunlight or moonlight in. My family had retired for the night. My two younger boys were asleep in one room, and my wife and I were fast asleep in a room next to them. My older son, fourteen, had his own pad upstairs in the attic. In the middle of the night someone tapped me on the shoulder—it was my older son standing next to my bed holding two Louisville Slugger baseball bats. I thought, *It's too late to play baseball; besides, it's too dark.* He said, "Dad, get up! Someone's trying to break into the door of our solarium."

I rolled out of bed and took one of the ball bats from my son, and we slowly and made our way through the dark house into the solarium. We could see by the moonlight shining through the solarium windows three grown men jiggling the doorknob and trying to force the door open. "What are we going to do, Dad?" asked my son.

I nervously replied to him, "If they break in, let's you and I hit each other with the ball bats." We nervously laughed. Thankfully, they also saw us inside with ball bats in hand and ran to their van and took off down the road. I followed them for two miles in my car until they pulled into a truck dock off the highway to hide. Fortunately, there was a phone nearby, so I called the police and they arrived quickly. I told them where they were hiding and said I was going home and to call me when they were captured. They called me later that night and informed me that the men were high on drugs and had been looking for money to buy more. Thank God for His protection–and for the Louisville Sluggers!

THOU SHALT NOT KILL

The Lord is with me; I will not be afraid.
What can mere mortals do to me?
(Psalm 118:6)

Early one Sunday morning I received a phone call at my home from the local chief of police. He wanted me to meet him at the church and would explain once I got there. So I hurried down to the church office, and there waiting for me were four officers: the chief and four plainclothes policemen–and they were packing heavy! The chief informed me that they had reason to believe there would be an attempt on my life as I preached the morning message.

We all agreed that this would be a good time to preach on "Thou shall not kill"!

The bulletproof vest they brought for me to wear was too small, and anyway I did not want to alarm the congregation. The officers secured all the side entrances so that the only doors accessible were the main entrance doors, where the police chief and another officer would be guarding in plain clothes. Two other officers would be patrolling the parking lots. Only my head usher and I knew what was going on that morning.

It seems that a woman who had recently visited our church and had responded to an altar invitation to accept Christ as her Savior went home and kicked out her live-in boyfriend. He blamed me for breaking up their relationship. In a rage he destroyed her car on Saturday night by ramming it with his truck and promised her that I would be shot dead in front of my congregation on Sunday as I preached from the pulpit. The police chief knew this man had a violent background and feared for my safety.

Thankfully, the would-be assassin did not show up that Sunday morning. However, he began sending me threatening letters through the mail advising me to watch my back, that he was coming. Our church office had to be locked down for the next several months. Finally, word came that he had left the state, and eventually things returned to normal. No one said this job would be easy—that's why pastors make the big bucks.

ABOUT the AUTHOR

Dan Walters answered the call to preach in 1977 at age thirty-one. He left secular employment in 1979 after fourteen years with the Ford Motor Company to enter full-time ministry. In 1982 Dan was ordained as an elder in the Church of the Nazarene and graduated from Mount Vernon Nazarene College that same year. He pastored churches in eastern Kentucky and southwestern Ohio. He retired in 2017 after almost thirty-three years as senior pastor of Tri-County Church of the Nazarene in Hamilton (West Chester), Ohio.

Dan has been married to his childhood sweetheart, Darlene, for fifty-three years. They have three grown sons, Danny Scot and his wife, Jenny; Darren Joel and his wife, Jody; and Devon Paul. They also have two wonderful grandchildren, Makenzie and Silas, who round out the Walters family. The family resides in West Chester, Ohio.

Dan Walters is co-author, with the late Stan Toler and Dan Casey, of an all-church discipleship program titled "Growing Disciples."

He also has developed a church leadership/church growth program called "The G.R.E.A.T. Church."

REV. DAN WALTERS AND WIFE, DARLENE, 2017

Made in the USA
Middletown, DE
01 May 2018